America's Road to Empire

AMERICA IN CRISIS

A series of eight books on American Diplomatic History

EDITOR: *Robert A. Divine*

America's Road to Empire

The War with Spain and Overseas Expansion

H. WAYNE MORGAN

John Wiley and Sons, Inc., New York · London · Sydney

To
Bud and Geri Lasby
James S. Chase
Norman D. Brown

Foreword

"THE UNITED STATES always wins the war and loses the peace," runs a persistent popular complaint. Neither part of the statement is accurate. The United States barely escaped the War of 1812 with its territory intact, and in Korea in the 1950's the nation was forced to settle for a stalemate on the battlefield. At Paris in 1782, and again in 1898, American negotiators drove hard bargains to win notable diplomatic victories. Yet the myth persists, along with the equally erroneous American belief that we are a peaceful people. Our history is studded with conflict and violence. From the Revolution to the Cold War, Americans have been willing to fight for their interests, their beliefs, and their ambitions. The United States has gone to war for many objectives—for independence in 1775, for honor and trade in 1812, for territory in 1846, for humanity and empire in 1898, for neutral rights in 1917, and for national security in 1941. Since 1945 the nation has been engaged in a deadly struggle to contain communism and defend the democratic way of life.

The purpose of this series is to examine in detail eight critical periods relating to American involvement in foreign war from the Revolution through the Cold War. Each author has set out to recount anew the breakdown of diplomacy that led to war and the subsequent quest for peace. The emphasis is on foreign policy, and no effort is made to chronicle the military participation of the United States in these wars. Instead the authors focus on the day-by-day conduct of diplomacy to explain why the nation went to war and to show how peace was restored. Each volume is a synthesis combining the research of other historians with new insights to provide a fresh interpretation of a critical period in American diplomatic history. It is hoped that this series will help dispel the illusion of national innocence and give Americans a better appreciation of their country's role in war and peace.

ROBERT A. DIVINE

Preface

JOHN HAY CALLED IT "The Splendid Little War." Theodore Roosevelt thought that it wasn't much of a war but it was the only one we had. The generation of Americans that fought it often thought it was a lark. It lasted a mere three months and was relatively cheap in human life. But it made legends in American military history and had profound diplomatic, economic, and political repercussions around the world. It dated American entry into the arena of world affairs. It was, of course, the Spanish-American War of 1898.

That war, small in scope yet large in consequences, has produced a sizable literature and is the subject of many historical debates. Was it preventable? Would a different president have freed Cuba by peaceful means? Who was chiefly responsible for war? Did public opinion or the needs of diplomacy force the conflict? Was it accidental or part of a larger and more conscious design? Few will deny the war's importance in American history. It brought empire in the Philippines and Hawaii. It made the nation feel like a world power. It served notice that Europe must reckon with American force in its own dealings.

This book offers a general introduction to the diplomacy that preceded the war, a very brief account of the conflict itself, and an explanation of the campaign for and against American expansion overseas. Briefly stated, my views are these: (1) The United States pursued a long, logical, and understandable peace policy toward Cuba, attempting to force Spain to reform the island and remove the issue from world affairs. The Spanish failure to do so provoked American intervention in 1898. (2) The

ix

United States had legitimate strategic, commercial, and humanitarian reasons for pursuing that policy and for being so deeply concerned over Cuba's fate. (3) The McKinley administration did not "surrender" to any sudden or inexplicable war hysteria after the *Maine* sank in Havana. The greatly overrated "yellow press" did not force the President to free Cuba. America's Cuban policy had held the threat of intervention since the days of Grant. By intervening in 1898, the McKinley administration merely accepted its inability to solve the Cuban issue peacefully. (4) The United States acquired Hawaii, the Philippine Islands, and other outposts of empire as part of a conscious program of extending American power into the arena of international politics and trade, and not by accident or default.

Such is the complicated story. I recount it in some detail, hopefully to avoid errors of simplification. Diplomacy is at best complicated, and the temptation to oversimplify and therefore distort is often strong. No war in American history has suffered from so many stereotypes and half-truths as that of 1898. In retrospect events seem far simpler than when they occur, and the view from within a policy-making machine is very different from that of later critical historians. I hope to give the reader a sense of policy development and of the thought and reaction that accompanied it.

Many historians have argued that the United States had no legitimate interests in Cuba; therefore, the policy that led to intervention was wrong. This retrospective thinking, involving little more at heart than a personal value judgment, is somewhat artificial. It deals less with what actually happened than with what a given scholar thinks should have happened. It makes little effort to understand the dilemmas, purposes, and problems that confronted policy makers at the time. To argue that the United States had no just reason to be concerned over Cuba's fate in 1898 is to hold that the United States had no legitimate interests in any other country at any time. Emotion, strategy, economics, and power politics logically focused American interest on Cuba. These forces figure in any nation's foreign policy and are understandably potent and logical. Nations presumably follow policies to further self-interest and to help other peoples. It is quite clear that this attitude prevailed among the great majority of Americans in 1898 and among the men who made diplomacy.

As the man responsible for foreign policy, President McKinley has suffered historically from many misunderstandings. The standard textbook stereotype still shows him as a well-intentioned bungler with no real policy who wished to avoid war but surrendered to public opinion. This view reflects more a lack of information than conscious distortion among scholars. McKinley's personality, his love of indirection, his refusal to conduct public diplomacy, and the shadowy nature of the forces surrounding his policy have made him seem the led rather than the leader. I hope the following pages show this view to be false. It seems more accurate and logical to trace the actual policy followed, and the forces that helped and hindered it, than to assume the United States had no reason to be concerned over Cuba or that the war was unnecessary.

A review of the policies and events that developed between 1895 and 1898 makes it clear that the administration faced several possible solutions to the Cuban problem in the crisis weeks that followed the sinking of the *Maine:* (1) It could continue to urge Spain to reform the island, attempt to quiet American public opinion, distribute relief in Cuba, and hope for the best. The administration did not do this because it had lost all faith in Spain's ability ever to solve the problem except by leaving Cuba. Neither the American people nor government could further tolerate the island's destruction. Spain refused to leave Cuba. (2) It could abandon Cuba, arguing that peace was preferable at any price and that no real issues compelled intervention. No one familiar with the facts can argue that this was possible. (3) It could seek a diplomatic solution during a "cooling off" period. Spain and the United States might have occupied the island jointly while working out a solution under a time limit. President McKinley offered a similar plan with himself as final arbiter, but Spain consistently refused to permit American mediation or peaceful intervention. A summit conference might have been called involving other powers. The United States did not consider this, since it would have involved the country in European diplomacy, would have found small favor among the American or Cuban people, and

would have prolonged the crisis with no real hope of success. (4)
The United States could serve Spain with an ultimatum, demanding that she free Cuba peacefully in a stated period of time or
face war. This in effect is what Congress did in April 1898. War
followed. The logical necessities of American interests and
Spain's long-demonstrated inability to end the rebellion or invoke
a genuine autonomy program forced this conclusion.

The war's results, usually labeled "imperialism" with no real
definition of the term, flowed logically from the conflict. Though
the opponents of expansion at the time considered acquisition of
foreign territory a radical new policy, it was not. It was an end
as well as a beginning, the culmination of at least a generation's
tendencies in world affairs. It involved altruism toward native
peoples considered unready for self-rule, the prospects of Oriental trade and influence, and the belief that America must behave
like the world power she was. Since this complex policy did not
really involve mere exploitation, I call it "expansionism."

I must say a final word of thanks to those who helped me write
this book. Much of the information presented here appeared in
a different form in my book *William McKinley and His America*
(Syracuse, 1963). Since writing that book I have changed and
extended many of my ideas, but I wish to thank that most generous of publishers, Richard Underwood, for permission to re-
print material here. Two friends, Robert Divine of the University
of Texas and Bill Gum of John Wiley and Sons, have helped a
good deal with editorial labors. Needless to say, what emerges
from the struggle is my responsibility alone.

H. WAYNE MORGAN

Austin, Texas
November 1964

Contents

MAPS

(Maps by Theodore R. Miller)

America's Road to Empire

CHAPTER I

"Cuba, Voluptuous Cuba"

S HORTLY AFTER THE CIVIL WAR the American government decided that its growing foreign relations required larger quarters. Early in President Grant's administration formal plans were
ready for a lavish new State Department building to be located
next to the White House. The huge structure was begun in 1871,
and by 1875 the south wing housed personnel of the diplomatic
service. The rest of the building rose slowly, for Congress was
stingy and only grudgingly doled out annual appropriations to fin-
ish it. The building was finally completed in the mid-1880's, taking its name from the executive offices it housed, State, Navy,
and War.

To symbolize the nation's wealth and growing power, the
architect found a lavish design that typified the taste of the Gilded
Age. The building's profusion of pillars, balconies, and windows,
all decorated with lavish detail, make "Old State," as it is now
called, one of Washington's most charming monstrosities.
Though now fallen into genteel decay, it still awes the visitor,
who finds the sinuous stairways, stained skylights, marble ceiling
molds, the 1572 windows, and ten acres of floor space elegantly
impressive. The building now has a double symbolism: it houses
hundreds of overflow personnel attached to the presidency; and
its original occupants have long since moved to much larger
quarters.

Government officials insisted that it would permanently house
the three great executive departments, which seemed logical in
the years between the Civil War and the War with Spain. Diplomacy in that era was rather informal, as were American diplomats. The Washington sightseer might notice the Secretary of

State cross the lawn to the White House on a mission involving a foreign crisis or perhaps merely a question of political patronage. The secretaryship of State was every administration's premier post, illustrious for its association with the presidency and the stature of its occupants. Presidents normally filled the post with an outstanding party member. It was often the refuge and reward for defeated presidential aspirants, who commanded respect, dispensed party patronage, and made foreign policy.

There was some irony, however, in reflecting that this post dealing with foreign relations was often important for largely domestic reasons. The diplomatic service was prestigious, but appointments were too often "gilt edged pigeon holes for filing away Americans, more or less illustrious, who are no longer particularly wanted at home."[1] Though every president managed to improve the diplomatic service, it was too easy for demagogues to convince many that it was all a waste of money. A latent distrust of conference and diplomacy runs through the history of a people who usually prefer action to talk. "What a pity it is that diplomacy is not more a career with us!" President Benjamin Harrison lamented as late as 1891.[2]

The diplomatic service mirrored these attitudes. In 1869 a penurious Congress allowed the State Department a mere 31 clerks; only by Herculean efforts did the President increase their number to fifty in 1881. Congress only gradually voted funds for specialized bureaus, and experts to staff them were difficult to find. American diplomats often behaved like the domestic politicians they were, though occasionally a distinguished man of letters went abroad to represent the United States. They wore no uniform, in respect to republican simplicity. As late as Theodore Roosevelt's administration, Secretary of State Elihu Root vetoed a suggested uniform, complete with ribbons and frills. Remarking that the congress would never tolerate such monarchial show, he suggested facetiously that the Department's emblem on such regalia be a sprig of mistletoe embroidered on the coattails.

---

[1] Cincinnati *Commercial*, November 20, 1877.

[2] Harrison to Whitelaw Reid, December 14, 1891, Whitelaw Reid papers, Library of Congress, Manuscripts Division, Washington, D.C. (abbreviated LC hereafter).

Though the currents of change were slow and often hidden, subtle forces carried the nation toward participation in world affairs, and the country transacted important foreign affairs during the Gilded Age. World news interested Americans, and every major newspaper in the country reported foreign wars, diplomacy, and events, though America was usually an observer, not a participant. No country so strategically placed, so rich in resources, and with so many diverse interests could remain isolated from that participation forever. In these years American representatives attended international conferences dealing with the silver question, postal rates, time zones, and literary copyright. Trade carried American ships to the earth's far corners. The Navy grew into a new fleet between the administrations of Arthur and Roosevelt. American explorers penetrated the jungles of Africa and the frozen polar wastes. Gradually, the nation acquired isolated outposts that symbolized this growing trend; coaling stations, cable landings, harbors passed under her jurisdiction.

In Latin America the United States enforced the Monroe Doctrine, looking upon the hemisphere as a special protectorate. A sharp diplomatic crisis occurred over Venezuela in 1895 and 1896 when a surprisingly bellicose President Cleveland forced arbitration of a boundary dispute on Great Britain and her Latin neighbor. In the years that immediately followed the War with Spain, the United States emerged as a full-fledged power, though she steadfastly pursued the traditional policy of independent action while sometimes cooperating with other nations. In those years America had friends but no allies bound by the formal ties of treaties or military agreements.

But for most Americans these negotiations and subtle movements, so tediously drawn out and often frustrating, held little of the allure that surrounded domestic party politics and public questions like the tariff, free silver, or the Southern problem. Although diplomats negotiated many important agreements and precedents, their labors were often buried in the statute books or congressional hearings. The country thought of foreign affairs largely in terms of "crisis diplomacy." Always addicted to quick action and lack of restraint, too many Americans considered diplomacy the last refuge of timidity.

Of all these foreign issues, Cuba captured the greatest public and official interest for the longest time. From the days of the "Ostend Manifesto" of 1854, Americans of all classes assumed a special relationship over Cuba. To them, Spanish rule there was a model of what the Monroe Doctrine ought to prevent. The island lay a scant hundred miles from Florida, and many said that destiny as well as common sense tied the two lands together. The island's strategic, commercial, and emotional ties to her northern neighbor were obvious.

The post-Civil War generation took pleasure in repeated Cuban revolts against Spanish rule. An oppressive political system, economic domination by the mother country, and cruel repression of attempted reforms forced the Cubans into revolt between 1868 and 1878 in the "Ten Years' War," and again in 1895. Each shock sent tremors north to stimulate ambitious men. To most Americans these struggles were freedom's birthpangs. To others, like William Randolph Hearst, they were the chance for enshrinement in the history books. For some they offered hope of economic exploitation in the island itself, political success at home in the United States, and emotional pride in America's mission and power abroad.

Demands for American intervention were often loud and persuasive to millions, but no president except Grant lent them an eager ear. He and the Republicans who supported his administration found Cuba alluring for many reasons. Intervention would undoubtedly please many people and take attention away from domestic failures and scandals. There was a genuine desire to free Cuba. And already there stirred in many quarters the desire for overseas expansion that would culminate in 1898. Every day's mail during most of his administration brought letters urging him to intervene in Cuba. "For God's sake let us go in, and Cuba, voluptuous Cuba, will be the reward," a Kentuckian wrote Grant. "People everywhere wish something to stir them up. Times are dull. A war with Spain would be very popular in this state."[3] Few remarks better illustrate war's unreality to that generation of Americans.

Though Grant seemed willing, Secretary of State Hamilton Fish headed a cautious faction that thwarted whatever desire to

---

[3] J. R. Dabney to Grant, January 11, 1872, Benjamin Bristow papers, LC.

free Cuba existed in the administration. He chose instead a firm policy of pressing reform upon Spain, the basic demand of all his successors. During the tedious diplomacy that followed during the Ten Years' War, Fish uttered phrases that sounded all too familiar to the public of 1895–1898. "It is now more than five years since the uprising," he reminded the Spanish, "and it has been announced, with apparent authority, that Spain has lost upward of one hundred millions of dollars, in efforts to suppress it; yet the insurrection seems today as active and as powerful as it has ever been."[4] Though his long efforts to compel Spain to accept American arbitration failed, the Secretary made it clear that American patience was not limitless. He also insisted formally that whatever Spain might do in the immediate situation, the United States would insist that she free Cuba some time in the future. In 1878 Spain purchased a specious peace with paper reforms. The fires of war and hate in the island never really died; they merely smoldered, ready to burst out at any time. Millions of Americans, of all political persuasions, took a consistent interest in freeing Cuba long before Hearst's yellow press exploited the problem. It was deeply ingrained in American consciousness decades before William McKinley took office.

Cuba was "The Ever Faithful Isle," for when Spain's possessions in the New World became independent in the early nineteenth century, she remained loyal to the mother country. In 1895, however, the Cubans rebelled again. In the months and years that followed, Spain poured men and material into her effort to suppress the outbreak that denied her apparent poverty and showed the deep attachments of pride, politics, and economics that tied her to Cuba. In Spain the people were poor, sharply divided by class allegiance, and sullen under the weight of political oppression, but alive to the echoes of an imperial past that surrounded Cuba's name.

In the quiet of ministerial conferences and official reports, many Spanish officials agreed that the Cuban war was too costly and even hopeless. Behind the ornate facade of Old World diplomacy lay little substance of power. But it would not do to utter

---

[4] *Papers Relating to the Foreign Relations of the United States* (Washington, D.C., 1874-1875), II, 1180 (abbreviated *For. Rels.* hereafter).

these truths aloud. The dynasty was weak, political parties bitter and fragmented. Pride was a powerful amalgam holding the machine together. To this stubborn pride, Spain added the irritants of official delay and domestic instability. The elaborate game of musical chairs that characterized Spanish politics meant periodic shufflings of portfolios, abandonment of policies half begun, veerings toward liberalism and then conservatism that baffled and angered both the American people and their government.

Though many Americans thought the Spanish were deliberately and unnecessarily obtuse, they had to oppose American efforts to free Cuba. Spain did not always consciously try to thwart American will, oppose peace, or compel the day of reckoning. But like her American foes, she had groups to appease, demands to fulfill at home, interests to protect abroad. Neither country had much flexibility in her situation, and the difficulties of both can be appreciated.

The casualty lists and exchequer reports mirrored the mother country's efforts to save Cuba. By the end of 1896 an estimated 150,000 Spanish soldiers had seen service in Cuba's jungles. By 1898 some 50,000 were dead, and another 50,000 disabled by disease and wounds. None could accuse the Spaniard of cowardice, but his bravery could not end the terrible war that dragged on year after year, or overcome the diplomatic inertia that delayed an arbitrated settlement. In Cuba the economy deteriorated. The island's exports to the United States, her principal customer, fell by half between 1894 and 1896. In the latter year, half the taxes collected in the island supported the Spanish war effort, and at the year's end exports to the north were a fourth of what they were in 1893. It was a fearful price for either country to pay, but set a pattern that deepened with time. Spain could have suppressed the rebellion only by a powerful military assault and domestic political unanimity beyond her means.

What threats, bribery, and war could not accomplish, fire and the machete might. On February 16, 1896, the new Captain-General, Valeriano Weyler, proclaimed the policy of reconcentration. If the rebels would not fight in the open field, he would herd their women, children, and old people into cities and towns, construct elaborate defenses, and systematically reduce the coun-

CUBA AND THE UNITED STATES

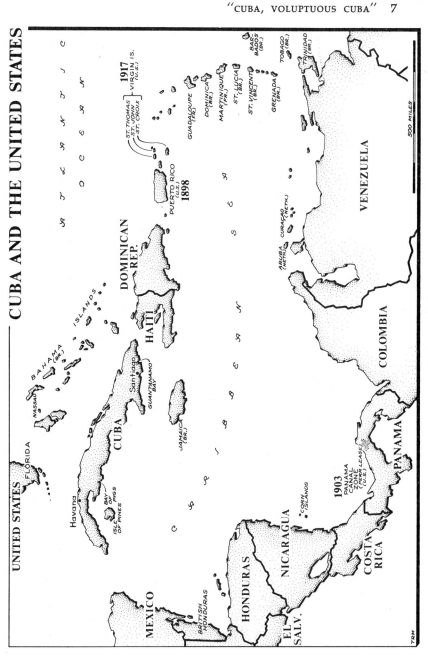

MORGAN MAP 1 W-1

tryside until it would not support the insurrection. It was a brutal method that inflamed American public opinion, the press, pulpit, and government. A later generation, inured to the prospect of total annihilation, may find this hard to believe; but that era's concept of war did not encompass the destruction of nonmilitary property, ravagement of whole provinces, and murder of non-combatants. New York newspapers titled Weyler "Butcher" and said succinctly: "Weyler has turned the island into a prison."[5] So pacific and patient a man as President McKinley said tersely in his annual message of December 6, 1897: "It [reconcentration] has utterly failed as a war measure. It was not civilized warfare. It was extermination."

Desperate but confident of ultimate American assistance, and deaf to false Spanish promises, the Cuban rebels fought on grimly. They commanded respect, a ready audience of millions, and financial and moral support in the United States; for Spain's demonstrated inability to settle the Cuban issue during the previous Ten Years' War predisposed most American feeling against her. Surveying his motley legions, ill-clad, poorly armed, Cuba's patriot leader Maximo Gomez could only say: "With these oxen we must plow."[6]

Cuba's agony inevitably and understandably aroused humanitarian sympathy in the United States. The American is generously and honestly endowed with the desire to relieve suffering and to extend to others what he considers the blessings of his way of life. Believing that his country is history's chosen child, he deems it not merely a right but a duty to give the best part of his heritage to the less fortunate. Some men fight for their country's boundaries or to add a province to their nation's domains. The American is more easily moved to liberate the provinces of the heart and mind. He is seldom repaid in gratitude, rarest of all human currencies. And such actions are often erroneous, rash, or averse to his own country's immediate best interests. But these feelings, so deeply and honestly a part of the nation's history and thought,

---

[5] See Joseph Wisan, *The Cuban Crisis as Reflected in the New York Press 1895-1898* (New York: Columbia University Press, 1934), 88 ff.

[6] Horatio Rubens, *Liberty: The Story of Cuba* (New York: Brewer, Warren and Putnam, 1932), 123.

have been the greatest single force in American foreign policy. Cuba in 1898 was a classic example of their operation.

A generation like that of 1898, unfamiliar with the horrors of war, innocent of the tangled responsibilities of world power, could not fail to heed the cry of oppressed Cubans, who wove into their appeals subtle reminders of special American responsibilities and interests in the hemisphere. Did the Monroe Doctrine selfishly protect some and oppress others? "It cannot protect American territory and at the same time surrender its unarmed inhabitants to the cruelty of a ferocious and despotic European power," Gomez reminded President Cleveland. "It must also extend to the defense of American society."[7] Such a call to arms seemed not merely logical but historically imperative to millions of Americans.

While emotion pulled many Americans toward the conflict, others had more practical reasons. The Spanish mistreated American citizens, stopped American vessels on the high seas, destroyed American property. Those with commercial and financial interests in the island found the endless rebellion disastrous. The torch lit the cane fields systematically, both to break the rebellion and for mere vengeance. Gomez destroyed property to keep the issue alive in the United States and to provoke American intervention. Clouds of smoke by day and flickering tongues of flame by night marked the island's progress into economic ruin.

Political repercussions in the United States were instant, crossing party lines, illustrating how potent the Cuban problem could be. At various times it was the only issue that united the disparate wings of either major party into a single cry, "Cuba Libre!" Like a contagion, the desire to free Cuba spread through American politics after 1895. Even so staid a man as Senator John Sherman of Ohio remarked that "no earthly power" would keep the United States out of Cuba.[8] Every session of Congress

---

[7] Gomez to Cleveland, February 9, 1897, in 55th Congress, 1st Session, Document 75 (Washington, D.C., 1897), 6. Strictly speaking, of course, the Monroe Doctrine did not apply in Cuba, since it offered no opposition to European colonies in the New World founded before 1823. But most Americans and Cubans then assumed that its anti-European sentiment fortified their desire to drive Spain from the hemisphere.

[8] *Congressional Record*, 54th Congress, 1st Session, 2244–2248.

saw many members of both houses introduce a variety of resolutions offering sympathy for Cuba, calling on Spain to yield, recognizing Cuban belligerency, or proposing some aid to the island's heroic revolutionaries.

Congress relished the belief that it represented the people's will. Its members had only to read a newspaper or thumb through daily mail to believe that the country wanted a free Cuba. Each day's sheets brought fresh details of the horrors of reconcentration, decrying the belief that anything but evil could come from Madrid, where ennui, deviousness, and pride sat enthroned behind smiling promises of reform. Through all the organs of public opinion ran the theme not of sordid self-interest but of redeeming Cuba with the promise of American freedom and democracy. The irony that so noble an end was often propagated by newsmen whose profession was lying impressed relatively few who read their wares.

But what Congress thought and what it could do in fact to free Cuba were two different things. Through the first stages of the Cuban rebellion, senators and representatives confronted the stolid figure of Grover Cleveland in the White House. Cautious and inflexibly determined to do the right thing, Cleveland proclaimed American neutrality in the conflict on June 12, 1895. He and members of his cabinet endeavored to prevent American embroilment by dissuading shippers from trading in Cuba, diverting embarrassing American loans from the island, and indirectly warning Americans not to flout the spirit of neutrality. Ever watchful of his prerogatives, Cleveland never permitted Congress to dictate or formulate policy. Any resolutions that body might pass, he held, merely expressed congressional opinion. He alone made foreign policy.

And what was that policy? The problem was acute and pressing, and no man of his integrity and awareness of American interests could ignore it. Neither he nor his Secretary of State, Richard Olney, ever recognized Cuban belligerency. That would invite further hostility from Spain, and perhaps cruelly prolong Cuban resistance in the false hope of American aid. They resorted to time-honored diplomacy: if only Spain would either end the rebellion, thus removing the issue from their care, or reform the island to everyone's satisfaction, there would be no need to intervene.

His policy of apparent aloofness brought Cleveland more than his share of poison pen letters, illustrating vividly that the issue was far from dormant or solved in the minds of millions. "I believe it is not the fear of a war with impotent Spain that stays your hand from the execution of justice," one correspondent railed at him. "It is your sympathy with tyranny."[9]

A policy was necessary, both to placate American opinion and to end the war in Cuba. On April 4, 1896, Olney forwarded to Madrid a comprehensive statement of the American position. Insisting that the United States had no designs upon Cuba, he asked only that the rebellion end. At the same time he listed the long-held reasons for American concern over Cuba: trade, strategy, and a desire to end the barbarous war. "That the United States cannot contemplate with complacency another ten years of Cuban insurrection, with all its injurious and distressing incidents, may certainly be taken for granted."[10] The Spanish reaction to this and similar statements from Washington, each of which grew firmer after 1896, was characteristic: "We must avoid any appearance of doing what we propose to do on account of foreign pressure."[11]

His state papers revealed Cleveland's firm purpose to safeguard American interests in Cuba and strong resolve not to permit an endless and devastating war in the island. In his last annual message, of December 7, 1896, he warned Spain in unusually strong terms that the United States could not maintain its "hitherto expectant attitude" forever. He included a time limit for ending the Cuban rebellion. If Spain failed within that limit, he clearly implied the United States would feel free to intervene. Not wishing to commit the new McKinley administration or risk a break in diplomacy, he finally omitted the paragraph, but reemphasized American interest in her Latin neighbor's fate. "The spectacle of the utter ruin of an adjoining country, by nature one of the most

---

[9] Quoted in Ernest R. May, *Imperial Democracy* (New York: Harcourt, Brace and World, 1961), 68.

[10] *For. Rels. 1897*, 540–548.

[11] Quoted in May, *Imperial Democracy*, 103.

fertile and charming on the globe, would engage the serious attention of the Government and people of the United States in any circumstances." He warned pregnantly: ". . . the United States is not a nation to which peace is a necessity. . . ."[12]

Cleveland left office before the problem culminated, but he outlined the basic policy his successor pursued. And in their answers to his offers of mediation and his steady insistence that the problem would have to be solved, the Spanish outlined their own intransigence: Cuba was their business, not that of the United States; Spanish victory would soon end the war and solve the whole Cuban problem; if the United States would remain neutral, the rebels would lose hope and surrender.

That Grover Cleveland inflexibly opposed American intervention in Cuba, and that had he been president in 1898 there would have been no war, is one of the most durable ideas in American history. But the record of his diplomacy shows he accepted the possibility of intervention. He opposed an unnecessary war and was anxious to negotiate a peace if possible. He hated congressional interference in diplomacy. He wisely counseled caution and deliberation from the press and people. But he clearly warned Spain that she could not trade on American patience. What he might have done in April 1898 is a fascinating if insoluble question. Faced with the wreck of Spanish promises, the destruction of American interests, the threatened dissolution of American politics, and Spain's demonstrated inability to reform Cuba, he probably would have acted as McKinley did.

Filibustering brought clashes between Spanish and American authorities. The long coastline, with countless coves and islands, afforded many debarkation places for Cuban sympathizers. Though the Spanish protested otherwise, both the Cleveland and McKinley administrations carefully controlled violations of neu-

---

[12] Secretary of State Richard Olney added some sentences to Cleveland's draft of the annual message in November 1896. The paragraph dealing with the proposed time limit read in the original: "It would seem safe to say, however, that if by the coming of the New Year, no substantial progress has been made towards ending the insurrection either by force of arms or otherwise, the conclusion that Spain is incompetent to successfully deal with it would be almost inevitable." See Olney papers, LC.

trality and rebuffed all charges to the contrary. "This charge is without any basis in fact," McKinley snapped in his annual message of December 1897. Though both Spanish and American agents checked suspicious cargoes in ports, some filibusters did make the run to Cuba, feeding a small trickle of supplies to the rebels and promising more to come. Of seventy-one known such expeditions, only about a third reached Cuba, and the exiles in New York and Washington admitted the Navy's efficiency.

The "yellow press" was a far more public and vexing problem to politicians and diplomats. Newspaper influence was politically alarming and grew as the crisis deepened. "Every congressman has two or three newspapers in his district, most of them printed in red ink, shouting for blood," one politician complained.[13] The sensational dailies did almost everything to increase their circulation and inflame the Cuban issue, causing widespread doubt about both their veracity and effectiveness. "The most alarming Cuban revolutions have occurred in New York for many years—in speeches," the staid New York *Times* said on February 27, 1895, ridiculing both the yellow press and jingo politicians.

By 1895, coincidental with the rebellion in Cuba, two powerful men worked on the New York newspaper scene, each determined to outdo the other in sensationalism. The ruthless Joseph Pulitzer poured his energy into the New York *World*, and William Randolph Hearst did the same for the *Journal*. Cost was no object and, as war fever mounted in 1898, these dailies lost money to run extravagant extras. Atrocity stories flowed north from Cuba steadily in 1897 and 1898. Vivid language, striking sketches drawn by men who never left New York, lurid details composed in bars and cafes mingled with the truth about Cuba until the whole fabric dazzled millions into a stunned belief. Reporters rescued damsels in distress and upheld the American flag on filibustering expeditions. Artists furnished pictures from the palm-fringed isle and toured incognito in the devastated cane fields and sickened cities that housed the *reconcentrados*. An elaborate system of spies and rumor mongers spread lies until one man suggested acidly that Hearst's reporters free Cuba.

---

[13] Frederick H. Gillett, *George Frisbie Hoar* (Boston: Houghton-Mifflin, 1934), 195.

It all had its effect, causing honest folk to wish for war's glories in a tropic setting. Even the administration noted it from time to time, though both Presidents Cleveland and McKinley, old hands at party politics, heavily discounted what little of the yellow press they read. In Washington and New York, the Cuban junta, composed of exiled revolutionaries and American sympathizers, fed rumor and information to friends in the press and Congress. Newsmen gathered in their rooms at the "Peanut Club," to eat peanuts and drink beer while swapping lies or the truth, depending on the day's doings. The junta was a clearing house for information and propaganda, and had it not been riddled with strife and short of funds, it might have been even more provocative in filibustering both in Congress and off the shores of Florida.

The power of the press in fomenting American intervention in 1898 was indefinable. The Cubans themselves held that, however valuable it was to them, it merely fed a public opinion that already existed. Newspaper pressure helped cause the war by keeping diplomacy unsettled in the face of mounting public opinion and ranting congressmen. Yet neither Cleveland nor McKinley assigned it first place among their woes. It is not too much to say that, had all other forces except the sensational newspapers been active in 1898, war would have come without the yellow press.

In all the welter of advice, pressure, and discontent, the role of business and economics was the least certain. Those with interests in Cuba preferred intervention; those without them usually did not. On the whole, business was probably not inclined to war. McKinley was elected in 1896 during the century's worst economic depression. Most business interests supported him and now asked only for peace and harmony to revive commerce. His primary mission was to restore prosperity. Who could foretell what complications might arise from intervention in Cuba?

The businessmen thought their viewpoint sound, but their opponents pilloried them as "the soulless sordidness which dignifies itself with the title business interests'. . . ." Wall Street's opposition to freeing Cuba made it "the syndicated Judas Iscariot of Humanity" to many. Millions of Americans could have agreed with the poet who wrote:

Shall half a gross of merchants—
The Shylocks of the trade—
Barter your heart, and conscience, too,
While freedom is betrayed?[14]

Pledged to negotiation and peace if possible, McKinley welcomed business support, but it was not an unmixed blessing. If he acted against it, he alienated the Republican party's most potent backers; if not, he alienated public opinion. In the end, with characteristic deftness, he helped bring business to his viewpoint.

And one added force loomed larger as McKinley took office, since most of its adherents were Republicans. A small but potent group of intellectuals preached the new doctrine of "expansion," playing on national pride by linking it with slogans of "manifest destiny'" and the prospect of acquiring foreign markets. Captain A. T. Mahan in the Navy; Whitelaw Reid, publisher of the New York *Tribune*; Theodore Roosevelt, soon to be Assistant Secretary of the Navy, all had voices and contacts in the new administration. John Hay, ambassador to England and later Secretary of State, envisioned an Anglo-American world understanding. If the public's interest in Cuba focused mainly on problems of morality and freedom, these men were more practical. They talked of larger navies, the prestige and virtues of world power, the significance of foreign possessions, and overseas markets. President McKinley did not read their thick and complicated books or their wordy articles, but he knew their names and they had access to him.

This was the complicated problem that occupied so much of Grover Cleveland's time and thought as he prepared to leave office. It remained unsolved, and the bitter election of 1896, revolving wholly around domestic issues, seemed to forebode a turning outward. Cuba would clearly be at the heart of McKinley's incoming administration. He inherited an old and complicated problem, woven of the tangled strands of economics,

---

[14] New York *Journal*, June 1, 1897; Sacramento *Bee*, March 11, 1898; Robert Walker, *The Poet and the Gilded Age* (Philadelphia: University of Pennsylvania Press, 1963), 196.

morality, power politics, and imperial policies. It would have to be met. Though he seemed to know little of it, Cuba was familiar to McKinley. It was so persuasive an issue that both party platforms in 1896 favored the island's freedom, implying clearly that if Spain would not surrender she must be expelled. Neither Cleveland nor McKinley could ignore the problem, for both knew that a hundred miles off Florida's coast, ragged and bearded men nightly toasted the health of the president of the United States, sure that sooner or later he would come to their aid.

CHAPTER II

Enter, Mr. McKinley

THE MORNING OF MARCH 4, 1897, dawned clear and cold, with a slight wind blowing across a Washington gaily decked for a presidential inauguration. "McKinley weather," the newspaper reporters called it, and it seemed to herald good times. William McKinley, who took the oath of office as President that day, had long been associated with harmony and prosperity. He had built his campaign for the presidency around a captivating slogan that made him "The Advance Agent of Prosperity." The election through which he so recently passed was one of the bitterest in American history, and in its tension symbolized the nation's long economic and social agony.

The man who took the oath in a firm voice at the Capitol's east front was no stranger to his audience. A veteran of long service in the national House where he represented his Ohio district as a faithful Republican, his name was a household word to most Americans long before he attained the presidency. He had devoted fourteen years in Congress and four years in the governorship of Ohio to advocating tariff protection, which his name symbolized in the McKinley Tariff of 1890. In those years he used tariff protection to foster a platform of economic nationalism that by 1895 made him the paramount contender for the White House. In 1895 and 1896 with the aid of his close friend and campaign manager, Marcus A. Hanna, later a senator from Ohio, McKinley fashioned a party program that stressed his own personal talents and economic nationalism. In hard-fought preconvention battles, he and Hanna routed leading party bosses to win the Republican nomination. In the bitter fight that followed against William Jennings Bryan and free silver, he brought to his side the business community and large blocs of labor and middle-class support to win a victory that stressed national development symbolized by a triumphant gold standard and tariff protection.

Personally attractive, looking every inch the President, McKinley bore beneath his dignity an affability and personal charm that made him widely loved and politically effective. He excelled in the personal interview, and had no taste for the written word. His leadership rested on unwritten understandings, woven from tireless appeals to the national good and party fealty. Many saw in him an amiable nonentity, an impression easily fostered by his deft dissimultion and his personal dislike of the limelight. Others knew him to be a man of great political skill and concrete commitments. So hard a judge as Grover Cleveland thought that his successor was committed to honest negotiation over Cuba, an impression that McKinley fostered in their formal interview a day before his inauguration. Cleveland was frank enough to say that he thought he left McKinley a war with Spain. And McKinley was honest enough to hope that he could do as well as Cleveland in avoiding war.

McKinley had the weakness of his talents. His lack of personal flair tended to blur both the man and his ideas. But he had many assets: personal acquaintance with almost every leading political figure of the day; a large body of public opinion committed to his support; control over his party and the ability to work well through congressional subordinates; and great personal talents at harmonizing conflicting views and persuading men to sacrifice personal gain for a larger national good. If he was not often bold, he was honest and skilful, endowed with the strengths of personal integrity and long political experience.

Many voted for McKinley in 1896, assuming that he and a triumphant Republican Party would free Cuba, or at least compel Spain to adopt more lenient policies. He presided over a party that traditionally favored overseas expansion. It was the home of James G. Blaine's Pan-Americanism, filled with spokesmen for widening economic penetration in the Orient and South America. Though he had seldom committed himself on issues of foreign policy, McKinley's record was generally liberal. Republicans from the East often spoke only for big business, with little interest in or knowledge of labor or agriculture. But that was never true of

McKinley. The uncertainties of Ohio's notorious politics, a wavering home district often gerrymandered against him by political enemies, and his own personality made him a leading spokesman of a "liberal" point of view while in Congress. He favored tariff protection, but by 1896 he was pledged to reciprocity, and together with Blaine was chiefly responsible for establishing that system in the tariff act of 1890 that bore his name. He knew of American interests in Hawaii and South America, was friendly to the American-Irish and -Germans, who were always outward looking, and was by no means ignorant of or opposed to international affairs.

As he left the inauguration, passing through cheering crowds, the new President knew the symbolism of the Capitol Hill he left behind. His party commanded slender majorities in both houses of Congress. They had beaten the silver heresy and its accompanying hysteria, but could the GOP meet the demand for intervention in Cuba as well? During his administration, as during Cleveland's, Congress was the focus of pro-Cuban sentiment, the clearing house of public opinion on the subject. The extensive debates of the spring session of 1896 impressed on everyone the power of congressional opinion. The lower house would now pose less difficulty because of Speaker Thomas B. Reed's iron hand and inflexible opposition to war. His ruthlessness combined with an acid wit and sarcasm to hold opinion in check until the very eve of conflict, though even then one man complained, "Mr. Reed has the members of that body bottled up so tight they cannot breathe without his consent."[1]

The most superficial poll showed, however, that the administration could not count on a firm congressional majority for a protracted peace policy. Unforeseen events might easily turn its small majority to intervention. In the Senate, where members were independent and powerful, a majority of both parties would have favored intervention at the slightest provocation. Democrats like Alabama's fiery old John T. Morgan brushed elbows with Republicans like Illinois' demagogic William E. Mason and Massachusetts' Henry Cabot Lodge at the headquarters of the Cuban

---

[1] H. S. Burtt to W. E. Chandler, March 28, 1898, W. E. Chandler papers, New Hampshire Historical Society, Concord.

junta in Washington. Their influence both on and off the Senate floor was powerful. They agreed to follow McKinley's lead in his effort to find a peaceful solution, but always retained the right to thwart his will in a crisis. McKinley somewhat offset this with his personal influence over Congress, and his work through powerful lieutenants like Hanna, Nelson Aldrich, and O. H. Platt.

McKinley called Congress into special session on March 15, 1897, to revise the tariff and fulfill his first campaign pledge. The Senate immediately burst into oratory about Cuba, always more interesting than tariff schedules. Resolutions recognizing Cuban belligerency and a variety of other things, all designed to force the President's hand or at least to impress congressional opinion upon him, circulated through the cloakrooms and on the floor. McKinley was not overly worried; his party control was firm. Senator Hanna told reporters that the President had the ace cards just now—prestige, public opinion, and patronage.

McKinley thought it best to treat the matter quietly, and recalcitrant or skeptical senators met at Secretary Sherman's home for an evening's talk over cigars and brandy. Some hinted that they would not pass a tariff bill if the administration throttled their Cuban resolutions. Administration spokesmen offered a familiar answer: conduct of foreign affairs was an executive matter, and any congressional resolutions would be mere opinion. The Senate passed its resolution, but the House obediently killed it.

Though partisans of a vigorous foreign policy took heart at McKinley's election, they sobered when they looked at the men around the new President. A wise politician, McKinley surrounded himself with other politicians; presumably they were open to pressure and persuasion, but they were not very excitable men. The premier post went to Ohio's conservative Senator John Sherman, a power in national politics for nearly half a century. It was a reward for long service, an attempt to capitalize on his great prestige, and a way of giving Hanna his Senate seat. It showed clearly, if anyone wondered, that McKinley would be his own Secretary of State, for Sherman was old and failing physically. McKinley's chief agent in the State Department was an Ohio friend, William R. Day, who filled the post of Assistant Secretary. Quiet, legalistic, cautious, he had the advantages of presidential trust and good personal judgment. "I see that the newspapers talk about the diplomacy of this administration as 'amateurish,'" Day once said with a slow smile, "and I must confess that it is."[2]

As the administration settled to a protracted tariff debate, many people wondered out loud about the new President's plans and talents. What, after all, did he know about foreign affairs? He had seldom discussed them in his public career. The campaign that made him President involved no foreign issue and he had remained silent on Cuba. In his inaugural address, McKinley touched foreign relations only in generalities, remarking merely that the country needed no wars of conquest, assuring listeners that negotiation over Cuba was best.

But McKinley was deceptive in this as in so many other things. He had many natural talents that helped him learn the methods and details of diplomacy quickly. Basic to all his actions was a deep sense of humanitarianism that made him look with horror upon events in Cuba. His concern for the national welfare bred the caution that continued Cleveland's policy of noninterference while negotiating. His adaptability, however, gave him a flexibility that Cleveland lacked. His habit of listening to and taking advice and of spreading responsibility for the policies he pursued laid careful groundwork for any ideas he followed. His extraordinary patience, and sensitivity to Spanish pride, made him prefer the charge of slowness to rashness. Though he delegated much authority, he retained a firm and careful control over all foreign policy. He read his mail to ascertain how the home folks felt. He talked freely with congressmen, smoothing ruffled feelings and oiling squeaking wheels. He tried to think for the long run as well as for the needs of the hour. Even critical jingos in his own party grew to respect his work. ". . . I think he could be depended upon to deal thoroughly and well with any difficulty that arises," Theodore Roosevelt condescended.[3]

McKinley bought at least a moment's respite from the expan-

---

[2] Quoted in Samuel F. Bemis, *American Secretaries of State and Their Diplomacy* (New York: Knopf, 1929), IX, 29.

[3] Henry Cabot Lodge, *The Correspondence of Theodore Roosevelt and Henry Cabot Lodge*, 2 vols. (New York: Scribner, 1922), I, 277.

sionists by turning first not to Cuba but to an older and less explosive problem, the annexation of Hawaii. The Sandwich Islands, as that generation knew them, summoned up visions of girls in hula skirts, fields of sugar cane, and pineapples. Though long an independent kingdom, their close relation to the United States was obvious. In return for special tariff rates on their exports, the islanders granted naval bases and trading privileges to the mainland. As early as the 1880's some American diplomats called the islands, as James G. Blaine put it, "the key to the dominion of the American Pacific. . . ."[4]

In 1893 the dominant Americans in Hawaii, mainly businessmen and missionaries, overthrew the monarchy and negotiated a treaty of annexation with the retiring Harrison administration. When he entered office in 1893, Cleveland withdrew the treaty because Americans had directed the revolution against the people's wishes. There the matter languished, despite several investigations, until McKinley took office. Cleveland really hated the manner rather than the thought of annexing Hawaii. "I do not now say that I should hold annexation in all circumstances and at any time unwise," he told Carl Schurz.[5] Why risk the problems of annexation when the United States so easily controlled the islands with the levers of trade and sentiment?

McKinley submitted a new annexation treaty to the Senate in June 1897, but remarked confidently to Carl Schurz that he would tolerate "no jingo nonsense in my administration."[6] Though he noted that the treaty was a logical continuation of older Republican diplomacy rather than a new departure, he did not push it. Realizing that its unfinished status would satisfy some expansionist sentiment, and unwilling to add the burden of a fight over it to his delicately balanced Cuban policy, he preferred to wait upon events. But through 1897 and early 1898, he obviously sympathized with the idea. He appointed an avowed

---

[4] James G. Blaine, *Political Discussions* (Norwich, Conn.: Henry Bill, 1887), 396.

[5] *Speeches, Correspondence and Political Papers of Carl Schurz,* 6 vols. (New York: Putnam, 1913), V, 133–134.

[6] Claude Fuess, *Carl Schurz* (New York: Dodd, Mead, 1939), 349.

annexationist as minister to Hawaii, and was concerned about
Japanese infiltration into the island's population. He looked upon
the Hawaiian problem as part of a general Oriental policy that
would carry American diplomacy and economic interests all the
way to China.

But Cuba remained uppermost in his mind, and he could not
formulate any policy there without accurate facts. He relied upon
two men for most of his information, the minister in Madrid,
and the consul-general in Havana. In the latter post, he inherited
one of Cleveland's most colorful appointees, Fitzhugh Lee. Addicted to strong cigars, tall talk, and white suits in which he
perspired partly from overwork and partly from high temper,
the mustachioed Confederate brigadier claimed the Great Lee as
an ancestor and had powerful friends in the Democratic Party.
He worked assiduously for his country's interests, but never
hid his desire to free Cuba. No Cuban languished in a Spanish
jail if he could prove his American citizenship, and Lee's hurrying
fat figure was a familiar irritant to Spanish officials. Cleveland
often doubted his judgment, complaining that he liked "the style
of rolling intervention like a sweet morsel under his tongue."[7]
But if he was outspoken, Lee was honest; he understood how
much McKinley would rely on him. The President thought of
replacing Lee, but such a move might give the Spanish the false
impression of a change in policy. He kept Lee at his post and
resolved to discount his reports if necessary.

The embassy in Madrid posed more problems. McKinley retained Cleveland's appointee, Hannis Taylor, while looking for
his successor. It was no easy task, and many criticized his delay;
but again the President was buying time. He talked to many
prominent men, urging upon them the necessity of the hour
and appealing to their patriotism. He needed a man in Madrid
whom he could trust, someone with patience and judgment. He
was candid to those he interviewed; the mission might be a failure, but they must do their best. He remarked significantly that
"if nothing could be done with Spain, he desired to show that he

---

[7] Allan Nevins, *Letters of Grover Cleveland* (Boston: Houghton-Mifflin,
1933), 448.

had spared no effort to avert trouble."[8] Not many men wanted the thankless task, but Stewart Woodford finally bowed to the President's persuasion. A distinguished lawyer, New York Republican, and officeholder under several presidents, he had tact, ability, and patience. McKinley trusted his judgment, and the new Minister arranged to send his chief extensive unofficial reports as well as official dispatches.

As Woodford prepared to leave for Madrid in the summer of 1897, McKinley had to formulate a public statement of Cuban policy. His first attitude was noncommittal, reflected in the generalities of his inaugural address. He excused the delay by talking of the pending tariff law, political patronage, and other official duties. Senator Cushman K. Davis, an expansionist from Minnesota and chairman of the Senate Foreign Relations Committee, stated the limits of the President's apparent policy in the bland remark that "the President will use his power to stop the bloodshed insofar as he can without involving the United States in war."[9]

The public did not receive this news enthusiastically, when every day's paper brought stories of atrocities and violations of American rights in Cuba. The President could not be idle; inaction might be worse than rashness. But he wanted information. He thought of sending Day to Cuba on a fact-finding mission, but decided he could not spare him. He finally dispatched a political friend, William J. Calhoun, who publicly investigated the death of an American citizen. Privately, he reported to the President on everything he saw in Cuba.

While McKinley went his rounds in Washington, Calhoun toured unhappy Cuba. In mid-June, he was back in the national capital; and on June 22, he sent the President his formal report. On the whole, he remarked, "The island is one of the most unhappy and most distressed places on the earth; . . ." He talked freely with Cubans and Spaniards in all walks of life, and they confirmed the clear evidence of brutal warfare. The Spanish insistence that Weyler and reconcentration were ending the rebel-

---

[8] Memorandum dated May 1897 in John Bassett Moore papers, Box 1, Library of Congress, Manuscripts Division, Washington, D. C. (abbreviated LC hereafter).

[9] New York *Times*, May 22, 1897.

lion "is more theoretical than actual." He placed no faith in official Spanish promises of reform. In the eyes of sullen Cubans, and on the face of the devastated land itself, he not only read the rebellion's progress, but the likelihood of its continuation. In some provinces the war was dormant, but it might "be likened unto a smoldering fire; the moment there is any relaxation of the attempt to suppress it, the flames will break out again with renewed fury."

He offered the President no real hope that the Cubans and Spaniards would compromise, or that autonomy could either be instituted or work. The island had been "the football of Spanish politics" too long for the Cubans to trust the mother country's promises. The Cubans were bitter at Spanish domination of the civil service, the economy, and the professions. He agreed with Consul-General Lee; ultimate American intervention offered the only real hope of pacifying and developing Cuba.

He included in his report a graphic description of the terrain that confirmed his judgments:

> I travelled by rail from Havana to Matanzas. The country outside of the military posts was practically depopulated. Every house had been burned, banana trees cut down, cane fields swept with fire, and everything in the shape of food destroyed. It was as fair a landscape as mortal eye ever looked upon; but I did not see a house, man, woman or child, a horse, mule, or cow, nor even a dog. I did not see a sign of life, except an occasional vulture or buzzard sailing through the air. The country was wrapped in the stillness of death and the silence of desolation.

If McKinley needed any added judgment to confirm his own belief that the war must stop, Calhoun's report furnished it.[10]

While Congress talked and he weighed the evidence of Cuban misfortune, the President must often have counted up his frustrations. The most remarkable aspect of his diplomacy was its lack of public focus. Cuba was obviously foremost in his thoughts, yet he never clearly defined what he proposed to do about it. Fearing

---

[10] Calhoun's report, dated June 22, 1897, consists of 22 typed pages, and is filed in Special Agents Reports, Vol. 48, Record Group 59, National Archives, Washington, D. C. (abbreviated NA hereafter; collections are organized in this depository by RG numbers).

to add impetus to the issue by discussing it, he followed his customary silence. All who met with him noted that he listened rather than talked. In all his personal correspondence, the word "Cuba" is never mentioned.

He thought for a time that he might solve the problem easily; perhaps the United States could buy Cuba, and then oversee her independence while the Cubans repaid their friends to the north. He sounded out visitors and set small rumors afloat. But the project came to nothing. Spain's answer had been heard many times and from many sources: "Spain is not a nation of merchants capable of selling its honor."[11] While the summer wore away, the President practiced his seasoned calm, talking in generalities in private, saying nothing in public. He thought he could remain above the battle, thus able to rally support if and when crises came. The danger was that he seemed inactive. He must accomplish something before Congress assembled in regular session in December or the public might turn against him.

From Havana Lee sent a steady stream of reports and complaints northward. In March he answered a query from Day on conditions in the island and outlined the position to which he clung until war came, and which in retrospect was a fair judgment: the rebels could not beat the Spanish, nor could the Spanish beat the rebels; the war would drag on until Spain was financially bankrupt or another power intervened; meanwhile the conflict would devastate the island and its people. He flatly denied that autonomy would work or that Spain would grant self-government. A month later he indicted the Spanish bitterly. "No one can fully appreciate the situation without being here in person."[12]

The President managed one policy that pleased everyone. On May 24, in response to a special message, Congress appropriated $50,000 for suffering American citizens in Cuba. Lee distributed the money through his offices. Though reports of starvation and destitution among American citizens of Cuban extraction were doubtless exaggerated, no one questioned the island's general tragic condition.

The news from Spain that summer seemed equally disheartening. The usual cabinet crisis did not produce men favorable to

---

[11] Washington *Post*, May 25, 1897.
[12] Lee to Sherman, April 20, 1897, Consular Letters from Havana, RG 59, NA.

the American position. A movement against the arch-conservative premier, Canovas del Castillo, failed, and the Queen Regent's support of the government made Minister Taylor lose hope. "All who were hopeful of amicable settlement on the basis of concilia- tion [are] profoundly discouraged," he cabled home.[13] He held out one small hope; the summer's abeyance in the fighting sharp- ened distaste for its resumption in the fall, and Canovas was growing unpopular at home.

In Cuba matters seemed even less sanguine. The President's great hope was an autonomous Cuba within a Spanish empire. Canada was often suggested as the model. But Lee and other observers thought this a false ideal, based on poor understanding of the Spanish character. "No one who is well acquainted with existing conditions now has any hope that Spain can grant reforms *approximating*, even, to Canadian autonomy, such as is so often mentioned."[14] Official Spanish failure to take these proposed reforms very seriously only added to rebel determination to succeed.

In view of all these doubts and confusions, McKinley decided not to delay a formal dispatch to Madrid until Woodford's arrival. On June 26 he forwarded over Sherman's signature the first official statement of his Cuban policy. The note took high ground, arguing in traditional American fashion that the rights of human- ity exceeded the rights of states. The new administration's demands were clear: revocation of reconcentration, rapid pacifi- cation of the island, measures to care for the populace, and permanent reform of the island. The President did not deny Spain's right to suppress the rebellion, but pointed out that his country had both tangible and intangible interests in Cuba. The most repugnant feature of the rebellion was the method of warfare: ". . . against the cruel employment of fire and famine to accomplish by uncertain indirection what the military arm seems powerless to directly accomplish, the President is constrained to protest, in the name of the American people and in the name of common humanity."

Neither the tone nor the words could have pleased Spanish ears. It sounded like Cleveland, and in places was even firmer:

---

[13] Taylor to Sherman, June 6, 1897, Dispatches from Spain, *ibid*.
[14] Lee to Day, June 8, 1897, Consular Letters from Havana, *ibid*.

He [the President] is bound by the higher obligations of his representative office to protest against the uncivilized and inhumane conduct of the campaign in the island of Cuba. He conceives that he has a right to demand that a war, conducted almost within sight of our shores and grievously affecting American citizens and their interests throughout the length and breadth of the land, shall at least be conducted according to the military codes of civilization.[15]

McKinley always included in his Cuban diplomacy a firm threat of intervention, and he was not pushed into war by public opinion or the yellow press when the final break came. He admitted that Spain must have time to reform Cuba, but he clearly insisted that the United States would not tolerate a prolonged conflict. He could not recede from this position once taken, a fact that did not escape his notice. It may well have determined all that followed, for he permitted himself the right to judge Spain's conduct and to set the speed with which she made progress. American diplomacy insisted on the methods to be employed in Cuba, but took no responsibility for them. While assuring both the Spanish and Cubans of American neutrality at the moment, it held the threat, or prospect, of intervention over both. McKinley's diplomacy was simply a logical extension of Cleveland's, consisting of steadily tightening the screws of diplomatic pressure. The implicit danger was that Spain would fight out of the corner into which she backed.

Spain's reply was not at once forthcoming, for speed was never among that country's virtues. Late in August, Enrique Dupuy de Lome, Spanish minister in Washington, transmitted his government's formal reply to the State Department. It breathed all the *hauteur* and truculence that Spain accorded American diplomacy regarding Cuba. Its substance was simple: Spain reserved to herself the right to determine the means of dealing with Cuba; the war was ending; the rebels could have peace whenever they wished merely by asking for it. It held out no hope that Spain would either modify her methods or attain her ends.

---

[15] *Papers Relating to the Foreign Relations of the United States* (Washington, D. C., 1897), 507–508 (abbreviated *For. Rels.* hereafter). In discussing legal problems surrounding the Cuban issue with the State Department's expert on the subject, John Bassett Moore, Day left the impression that the President "probably was thinking" of the possibility of intervention throughout 1897. See Diary-Memoranda, 1897, Moore papers, LC.

Meanwhile Woodford moved toward Madrid with deliberate slowness. On August 8 Canovas was assassinated. A successor might be more congenial. The new Minister stopped in London, where he talked with John Hay, soon to be Secretary of State. "General Woodford has arrived with his able and efficient staff," Hay wrote a friend. "He will stay a while here and a while in Paris, which will create the impression on the suspicious *hidalgo* that he is in no particular hurry to steal his islands."[16] In Paris Woodford sounded opinion from American diplomats on the continent, and concluded that "The Powers" were no real threat despite their ties to Spain through finance and monarchical sympathy. All the while he pondered the delicacy of his mission. It was his duty to make the Spanish understand that the United States did not wish to take Cuba; the President wanted to mediate the conflict on mutually agreeable terms. He would not recognize Cuban belligerency, but demanded speed.

By September Woodford was in Madrid, seeing the Old World sights, attending bull fights, settling to new tasks in his embassy building. He was charming and courtly, and was well received in social circles. But tact did not conceal his frankness as he tried to impress on Spanish officials the need for action. His surroundings confirmed his old suspicion that the task was hopeless. Underneath all the courtesy he sensed both a torpor and a defiance that boded ill for the future. "I have little hope of a peaceful solution, but am doing the best I can to get peaceful results," he cabled home.[17] After his first impressions had settled in his mind, and when preliminary talks with the Spanish were over, he was even more depressed. The government would play the cards of delay as long as it held them, he reported; Spain had no real Cuban policy. Like Mr. Micawber, she was only waiting for something to turn up. "It is a hand to mouth policy."[18]

Though Woodford thought that de Lome fed Madrid's dependence on delay by presenting McKinley's public silence as weakness, the President refused to conduct public diplomacy. He

---

[16] John W. Foster, *Diplomatic Memoirs*, 2 vols. (Boston: Houghton-Mifflin, 1909), II, 279–280.

[17] Woodford to Sherman, September 29, 1897; to McKinley, September 22, 1897, Vol. 131A, Dispatches from Spain, RG 59, NA.

[18] Woodford to McKinley, September 24, 1897, Vol. 131A, *ibid.*

was far from inactive. He fed a steady stream of cables to Madrid, advising, exhorting, asking for information. Late in September, Woodford renewed the President's formal tender of good offices. If Spain refused, he said, she must understand that the United States would feel free to change her policy. The offer was not, of course, pro-Cuban.

Canovas' death disrupted Spain's always precarious politics, and Woodford had delayed his arrival while an interim ministry prepared the way for the new Liberal cabinet. On October 4, 1897, Praxedes Sagasta, whose party had often criticized Canovas' harsh colonial policies, came to power, and for a moment many felt a fresh breath of air. Perhaps there was hope for a change of policy.

Woodford continued to exercise his justly appreciated courtesy, sounding official and unofficial opinion. Explaining the proposed autonomy scheme was his most difficult task. To the Spanish it looked like independence; to the Cubans it sounded like Spanish rule made even more devious. "I doubt whether the Spanish official mind comprehends real autonomy as Englishmen and Americans would understand autonomy," Woodford wrote home. "I doubt whether Spain could give in theory or enforce in fact such autonomy as Canada has."[19] It was the first of much cold water that washed the glamor off autonomy.

On October 26 the new cabinet delivered a comprehensive reply to past American notes. Though refusing presidential mediation, they agreed to speed up the campaign, employ humane methods, and grant some kind of autonomy. This fortified a major breakthrough for McKinley, who in October had received assurances that Madrid would recall the hated Weyler. Day had taken the chance to turn the screw again, telling de Lome that nothing could extend this apparent change of policy more than an end to atrocities in Cuba. From Madrid Woodford congratulated his chief at home, for as November opened it seemed that a whole new policy would be set in motion. Perhaps the President's peace plan would wear the crown of success after all.

In Washington Minister de Lome found the break in the cloudy relations somewhat irritating. Worldly wise and cynical, though

---

[19] Woodford to Sherman, October 16, 1897, *For. Rels., 1898,* 581.

an able and experienced diplomat, de Lome did not want to lose Cuba. Nor did he appreciate McKinley, whose genial charm seemed as irritating as his success in dealing with Madrid. But if the President felt the ice in de Lome's demeanor, he said nothing; grudges were not among his mental baggage. Whatever chill existed, he continued to greet the haughty Spaniard with every courtesy. In mid-November the President extended special social greetings to the Minister. His hand outstretched in warm welcome, his face wreathed in smiles, McKinley congratulated de Lome on what he called their joint success, expressing both the hope and the confidence that once begun on a new departure, Sagasta could not turn back.

The Spanish ministry seemed to fortify this hope. In November it promised that the Queen Regent would shortly proclaim extensive reforms in Cuba. The concentration camps would end, Weyler would return to Spain, autonomy would be instituted. Woodford quickly saw that the significance of such a policy was its mere beginning. "The Ministry have now entered upon their path of promised humanity, reform and autonomy. . . . If they should ever attempt to turn back or evade the logical results of what they now do, they will practically break their pledges to Cuba and to the United States. This would not only justify but might compel intervention."[20] He was dealing in prophecy.

But for now he tried to be hopeful. On November 25 the Queen Regent formally proclaimed the long-awaited Cuban decrees, outlining a comprehensive and complex autonomy scheme. To those who looked closely, however, it was not autonomy at all. Spanish appointees would dominate the proposed Cuban assembly, whose acts were at the mercy of a Spanish governor. All ultimate authority remained with the mother country. It was a house of paper. The New York press dismissed it as a hodgepodge made up for publicity. The administration remained silent; but in his annual message of December 5, 1898, after the war was over, McKinley said the scheme had disappointed the administration. It was not real autonomy; it never worked, the Cubans never accepted it; it did not stop the war.

---

[20] Woodford to Sherman, November 13, 1897, to McKinley, November 14, 1897, Dispatches from Spain, RG 59, NA.

Though Austrian by birth, Maria Christina acted as Queen Regent for her young son Alfonso XIII with all the formality of a Spanish monarch. Unlike some of her ministers, she seemed to prefer harmony with the United States, for she knew that war might topple her throne. Woodford thought her charming and reasonable, but her power was limited. In the tortured language of royal diplomacy, she told Woodford that Weyler had friends. Though she did not press the point, Woodford knew that many Spaniards preferred war to peace; defeat with honor was better than surrender. Weyler had not returned to Spain in disgrace. Crowds of cheering well-wishers met him at Barcelona, waving flags and chanting slogans that men in another hemisphere had hated.

In Havana General Lee made his endless rounds, protesting the treatment of American citizens, noting that whatever Madrid promised about autonomy, Cuba heard nothing of it. To his superiors he reiterated his single theme: Spain could not reform the island if she wanted to; intervention was the only ultimate answer. For himself, de Lome had somewhat similar thoughts in Washington. In December he cabled home: "My opinion has not changed in any respect. So long as a government is not formed in Cuba, and until the decrees are put into effect, the situation must remain expectative."[21] Delay, Spain's oldest weapon, might serve her purposes again. But time was running out, for Congress was now on the President's doorstep, ready to hamper his movements at every turn.

December's first snows brought congressmen straggling into the capital. They longed to turn to Cuba now, for the tariff no longer intrigued them and the Republicans lacked both the majority and the will to open the festering currency issue. Though the administration's congressional lines seemed firm around men like Reed and Hanna, McKinley's silence irritated many radicals. His apparent success in dealing with the new Spanish government made them more sullen.

---

[21] de Lome to Minister of State, December 16, 1897, *Spanish Diplomatic Correspondence and Documents 1896–1900: Presented to the Cortes by the Minister of State* (Washington, D. C., 1905), 52 (abbreviated *Sp. Corr.* hereafter).

De Lome foresaw a pacific annual message from McKinley, which might be a bad omen, for it would indicate his pleasure with progress toward Cuban autonomy that could not be reversed without a crisis. Congress was restive as a clerk read the President's message, asking for legislation on such things as tariff reciprocity and the banking system. The section dealing with Cuba seemed general, reciting the rebellion's history, counseling caution and watchful waiting. The President listed three alternatives to the present guerrilla war: neutral intervention, Cuban belligerency, and annexation. He would not recognize the Cubans, since they really had no organized government in the island. He spoke of the last alternative bluntly: "I speak not of forcible annexation, for that can not be thought of. That, by our code of morality would be criminal aggression."

He dismissed Spain's usual complaint that the United States did not enforce its neutrality laws with a curt aside. He would wait and see about the new program set in motion from Madrid. "It is honestly due to Spain and to our friendly relations with Spain that she should be given a reasonable chance to realize her expectations and to prove the asserted efficacy of things to which she stands irrevocably committed." But he included two strong paragraphs that should have given Spanish officials pause:

Throughout all these horrors and dangers to our own peace this Government has never in any way abrogated its sovereign prerogative of reserving to itself the determination of its policy and course according to its own high sense of right and in consonance with the dearest wishes and convictions of our people should the prolongation of the strife so demand.

If that was not clear enough, he added an injunction for speed:

The near future will demonstrate whether the indispensable condition of a righteous peace, just alike to the Cubans and to Spain as well as equitable to all our interests so intimately involved in the welfare of Cuba, is likely to be attained. If not, the exigency of further and other action by the United States will remain to be taken. When that time comes that action will be determined in the line of indisputable right and duty. It will be faced, without misgiving or hesistancy in the light of the obligation this Government owes to itself, to the people who have confided to it the protection of their interests and honor, and to humanity.

The implication was clear. Spain must act at once or the United States would intervene.

Reaction was swift if not sure. The message's pacific ring irritated many jingo Republicans as well as Democrats. Ohio's Republican Senator J. B. Foraker, New Hampshire's expansionist Republican Senator William E. Chandler, Illinois' "Billy" Mason all thought it weak. Ex-Minister Taylor frankly called it pro-Spanish, and constituents showered congressmen with protests. "His Cuban policy is cowardly, heartless and idiotic," a friend wrote Secretary of War Russell Alger. "McKinley is a Chinese statesman."[22] From Spain Woodford reported that the government appreciated the President's patient tone. Informal reports said that the talk behind ladies' fans at court and at the bull ring among the people was more hostile to American threats and pressures.

In Havana General Lee fumed with frustration, caught between Spanish delay and what he thought was an unreasonable policy in Washington. As if to supplement the President's message with deeds, Day arranged to have warships on call at Key West. If revolution or trouble came, Lee could cable the letter "A" and the Navy would respond.

In Madrid Woodford explained that the President's patience was not limitless and that Spain must now move quickly to capitalize on whatever favorable public opinion existed toward her. McKinley himself would not outline an autonomy policy, but he expected Spain to formulate one without any further delay, "the scope and effects of which must remain to be judged by their realization."[23] The President, however, was willing to extend aid to Cuban sufferers; whatever the new year might bring, the old one still held death and misery for thousands in Cuba. As the call for relief went out, he urged Americans to respond, and anonymously sent $5000.

With almost a year of diplomacy behind him, McKinley faced 1898 with some misgivings. True, he had wrung many concessions

---

[22] Washington *Post*, December 7, 8, 1897; W. D. Sloan to Alger, December 8, 1897, Alger papers, William L. Clements Library, University of Michigan, Ann Arbor.

[23] Woodford to Minister of State, December 20, 1897, *Sp. Corr.*, 52 ff.

from Spain, but they were only promises, and Spain had bought American patience with that coin many times before. His very success would make the new Congress more impatient with both him and his foreign adversaries. What would he do if the uncommitted moderate sentiment among many Americans swung toward intervention?

But the President's success was not without either merit or friends. He would have appreciated a private letter that Senator Lodge wrote a friend who criticized the peace policy. Lodge was an expansionist, yet he did not favor an unnecessary war. "I do not feel that you are just to the President in regard to Cuba," he wrote. "By the firm attitude which he has assumed he forced the withdrawal of Weyler, the release of all the American prisoners, the revocation of the concentration edict and of the tobacco order. Spain having made all these concessions, he would hardly say that they should not have the opportunity to try to pacify the island by autonomy, and I think he has acted wisely in so doing."[24]

They were comforting yet dangerous words, for they said in effect that having gained a little the President must now gain a great deal more. If his plans failed, there was nothing left but intervention. The problem rested with Spain. Could she break the log-jam of empty promises in 1898, or was she fated to lose the Ever Faithful Isle?

---

[24] Lodge to Albert Griffin, December 31, 1898, Lodge papers, Massachusetts Historical Society, Boston.

CHAPTER III

Intervention

H AVANA IN 1898 BORE THE MARKS of its divided character. To
the casual visitor it seemed a charming if somewhat incon-
venient city. From this seat of imperial power expeditions had set
out to conquer an empire for Spain. From this same regal city,
arrogant viceroys and captains-general had ruled that empire.
In 1898 the city still boasted this air of decayed grandeur, but
it was uneasy in the midst of a crumbling world. Now within its
confines stood not a conquering army but a mere garrison, surrounded by the horrors of war and disease.

Havana was not Madrid, nor were the attitudes of its people
those of Spain. Conditioned by events and interests in Cuba, both
its civil and military officials saw things in a different light from
that in the instructions and dispatches from Spain. The military
officer who received a command in Cuba soon lost heart when he
surveyed the scene of battle. The civil administrator who decided
to save Cuba for Spain soon fell into laxness and defeatism upon
facing the ingrained delay and lack of insight in the island's bu-
reaucracy. From the somewhat seedy but still ornate government
palaces in Havana issued a steady stream of edicts and orders
intended to change Cuba to American satisfaction, but they seldom impressed even the printers. The whole city symbolized both
the fact and danger of Spanish pride.

Much of the problem was inherent. Spaniards born in the island ran the Cuban economy and the political system. Their interests and passions dictated greater stubbornness than that in
Madrid. They condemned Weyler for doing too little, not for doing too much. Loss of the island would mean loss of office to
them; their control over finance and the economy would end.

They clung largely to the past. Their opposition to autonomy, combined with the rebels' desire for total independence, fortified Lee's belief that reform was hopeless, no matter what intentions motivated Madrid.

American pressures only sharpened that sullen opposition during 1897, for the Spanish elements in Cuba were far more conscious of "Yankees" than was the home government. On January 8 Lee reported that reconcentration was as bad as ever. On that same date in Madrid Woodford repeated his tireless and by now tiresome warning that "the result must be wrought out in Cuba and by facts, rather than at Washington or Madrid and by negotiation."[1]

But the new year holidays brought a specious lull in the diplomatic tension, as Washington passed through its annual orgy of entertainments. The President was as hopeful as ever, smilingly assuring his visitors that he expected quick results from the autonomy scheme proclaimed on January 1. Lee was skeptical, and the President's hopes shattered on January 12, when the cables told of destructive anti-autonomy riots in Havana. First reports caused alarm for loss of life and property; but the President remained calm, remarking his mock surprise to callers "that the war should be beginning outside the White House, and [I] know nothing about it."[2]

But this trace of humor did not cover his uneasiness. Weyler's former soldiers had led mobs against newspapers and businesses favoring autonomy. If the army and other influential groups dared openly assault even the idea of Cuban autonomy, what hope was there for a negotiated settlement? In the days that followed, McKinley remained silent, but the Spanish Minister and other diplomats noted his marked coolness toward talk of autonomy and Spain's ability to end the war. The riots subsided quickly, but the discontent and opposition they symbolized shook him more deeply than anything had in 1897. Even de Lome sensed the President's changed demeanor, and felt a hardening of attitude throughout the administration. "The change of sentiment

---

[1] Lee to Day, January 8, 1898, Dispatches from Havana; Woodford to McKinley, January 8, 1898, Vol. 131A, Dispatches from Spain, Record Group 59, National Archives, Washington, D. C. (abbreviated NA hereafter).

[2] Washington *Post*, January 13, 1898.

has been so abrupt, and our enemies influenced by it, so numerous," he cabled Madrid, "that any sensational occurrence might produce a change and disturb the situation. . . ." He noted presciently that the riots had "produced deep disgust among the moderates and those disposed to accommodate differences."[3]

De Lome may have been somewhat aloof and formal—he was an Old World diplomat in an era that accorded diplomats much power and respect—but he was also a shrewd judge of men and policies. He felt the President's coolness and heard the rumors that McKinley had lost faith in Spain's promises and ability. Under the spur of great events, he cabled home a frank analysis of the situation. "The news from Havana is not improved," he noted. "If it continues it will cause the situation here to change. The sensational press is just as bad as it was in the worst period, and the government and Cabinet, although they have said nothing to me, seem to have lost all faith in Spain's success, and, to some extent, to have lost tranquility."[4]

In Madrid Woodford talked frankly with the Queen Regent, whose regal attitude softened under his candor. For the moment he lost patience. "Let there be no misunderstanding in your mind or in the mind of any Spaniard," he said. "General Weyler will never be allowed to land in Cuba again. The old conditions of barbarity can never be restored. Any attempt to return to the old methods of barbarity will be met by instant, effective, and final intervention."[5] The Queen assured Woodford that no such backward step was possible.

In Washington McKinley paused to assess a year's labors for peace. He did not know that de Lome had privately sneered at both him and the proposed autonomy scheme, saying flippantly that it existed "for the purpose of printing it in the newspapers."[6] Whatever the Spanish proposed to do, they now ceased to be the vital factor, for the Cuban rebels continued to spurn the auton-

---

[3] See *Spanish Diplomatic Correspondence and Documents, 1896–1900: Presented to the Cortes by the Minister of State* (Washington, D. C., 1905), 63–67 (abbreviated *Sp. Corr.* hereafter).

[4] *Ibid.,* 64–65.

[5] Woodford to McKinley, January 17, 1898, Vol. 131A, Dispatches from Spain, RG 59, NA.

[6] Walter Millis, *The Martial Spirit* (New York: Literary Guild of America, 1931), 35.

omy scheme publicly. In Cuba's jungles, Maximo Gomez' tattered army took new hope; only independence would suffice. This sentiment, together with the Havana riots and growing doubts about Spain's actual power in the island, gave McKinley pause. "There is no longer any doubt that the President of the Republic is very much impressed with Lee's statements regarding the failure of autonomy," de Lome cabled home in late January.[7]

McKinley still shrank from public diplomacy, and was content to control Congress through senatorial friends and Speaker Reed. Both defeated pro-Cuban resolutions that would have weakened his control of policy. For the moment he was relieved, but the pressure on Capitol Hill was growing. Late in January, at the annual diplomatic reception, McKinley went out of his way to greet de Lome. Against the background of colorful uniforms, the sound of music, and the flash of medals, the President made way for the Spaniard through other ranking ambassadors. "I see that we have only good news," he said, smiling. "I am well satisfied with what has occurred in the House, and with the discipline of the Republicans." He paused, as if to emphasize his words. "You, who comprehend this, will understand how strong our position is and how much it has changed and bettered in the past year; you have no occasion to be other than satisfied and confident." [8] De Lome never cared for "the Major," as domestic politics had titled McKinley; he was a rural politician in many ways, despite his personality and talents, but he was sincere and firm in pursuing his country's interests. This night, his voice had an edge of iron; if things were better, Spain must see that they did not worsen, he seemed to say underneath the polite diplomatic language.

If de Lome had a conscience it must have twinged as he rode back to his embassy through the dark streets. Perhaps even then he thought a moment of the storm that might soon break over him, for he remembered writing a letter. Unimpeachable sources now said in the first part of February that the letter was about to be published. It would end his career in a celebrated diplomatic incident.

---

[7] See Lee to Day, January 18, 1898, Dispatches from Havana RG 59, NA; *Sp. Corr.*, 67.

[8] de Lome to Minister of State, January 28, 1898, *ibid.*

The letter's history said much of the whole Cuban problem. Irritated by McKinley's calm yet warning annual message in December 1897, de Lome answered a query from a friend in Havana. About the middle of that month, he wrote Don Jose de Canalejas, a Spanish editor and politician touring Cuba. Secretaries handled Canalejas' correspondence, and a rebel sympathizer noted de Lome's return address, opened the letter, and forwarded it north to friends in the junta. In New York, loyal juntists with connections among the newspaper guild realized the letter's significance. A facsimile went to the New York *Journal*, and the text went to other daily papers.

The bomb exploded on the *Journal's* front page on February 9. Readers looked at the facsimile with surprise and read the arresting headline: "WORST INSULT TO THE UNITED STATES IN ITS HISTORY." Many might have thought de Lome's letter less repugnant than the rest of the paper; but it was from the Spanish Minister. To the casual reader and to most subsequent students, the letter's importance lay in de Lome's aspersions on the President and his message. His words found their way into all the history books:

Besides the ingrained and inevitable bluntness with which is repeated all that the press and public opinion in Spain have said about Weyler, it [the annual message] once more shows what McKinley is, weak and a bidder for the admiration of the crowd, besides being a would-be politician who tries to leave a door open behind himself while keeping on good terms with the jingoes of his party.

However interesting this description, it revealed all the arrogance of Spain's attitudes and the hollowness of her negotiations.

In the State Department, eyes lighted on the last paragraphs. Though the man on the street overlooked them, they were far-reaching in their implications. In the supposed privacy of the mails, de Lome stated his views on autonomy and the peace policy in general:

It would be very advantageous to take up, even if only for effect, the question of commercial relations, and to have a man of some prominence sent hither in order that I may make use of him here to carry on a propaganda among the Senators and others in opposition to the junta and to try to win over the refugees.

In an earlier passage he held that negotiation with the Cubans was fruitless, and hoped for a Spanish military victory to end the war and save Cuba for the mother country. To the diplomats in the administration and the moderates in Congress, the letter's meaning was clear: Spain was insincere in her policy.[9]

The juicy morsel unseated de Lome, who resigned before its release to the press. Popular outcry echoed across the country, and a little ditty jangled through the yellow press:

Dupuy de Lome, Dupuy de Lome, what's this I hear of you?
Have you been throwing mud again, is what they're saying true?
Get out, I say, get out before I start to fight.
Just pack your few possessions and take a boat for home.
I would not like my boot to use but—oh—get out, de Lome.

The letter was a godsend for the Cuban junta, one of whose members said candidly: "The de Lome letter is a great thing for us."[10]

The day it appeared, Horatio Rubens, a loyal juntist, took the document to Judge Day, who looked at it without comment. A Department expert first thought it a forgery, but finally agreed that it was genuine. Day asked to keep the letter and walked across the street to show it to McKinley. The President did not comment, except to ask why it had not been brought to him first. Rubens had not done so because he feared the tolerant McKinley would hush it up.

The President remained silent; to comment was beneath his dignity. De Lome would have to go, which was unfortunate, since a knowledgeable successor would be hard to find. He might have been imprudent at times, but he knew the ropes of Spanish politics and was an experienced diplomat. The President's silence was the best rejoinder; a lifetime in politics had inured him to slander. The moderate press generally lauded his dignified stand, but here and there an administration paper shifted away from his peace policy toward intervention. Privately, McKinley understood the letter's full significance and knew that de Lome's mere resignation would not suffice. Spain must disavow these sentiments at

---

[9] The translation is from *Papers Relating to the Foreign Relations of the United States, 1898* (Washington, D.C., 1901), 1007–1008 (abbreviated *For. Rels.* hereafter), and is used because of its official nature.

[10] New York *Journal*, February 9, 1898; New York *World*, February 15, 1898.

once. For Day's benefit he outlined on a scrap of paper what he thought such an apology should contain: "Expressions of pained surprise and regret at the Minister's reprehensible allusions to the President and the American people, which it is needless to say the Govt. of His Majesty does not share, and promptly disavows."

Like the mid-January riots against autonomy in Havana which badly shook the administration's belief in Spanish promises and abilities to reform Cuba, the de Lome incident was far more critical than it seemed. Behind the vociferous public outcry against the Spanish Minister's studied insult to McKinley lay deeper meanings that marked a further step toward American intervention in Cuba. The letter's slander on the President forbade further American public trust in Spain. It turned many moderate newspapers and individuals toward intervention. Its clear intimations that the autonomy scheme was false and a ruse to buy time further convinced administration policy makers that only intervention would solve the vexing and seemingly endless Cuban problem. De Lome's departure also created a crucial vacuum in diplomacy. His successor could not arrive for perhaps two weeks, and an able replacement would be hard to find.

Former Secretary of State Richard Olney, an architect of the policy of negotiation over Cuba, saw the affair's full importance. "Poor Dupuy [de Lome] must realize how much worse a blunder can be than a crime," he wrote his former chief, Grover Cleveland. "Here is his country practically unrepresented at Washington at a time when its interests demand a *persona grata* at our capital more imperatively than ever before." He stated clearly and forcefully what the Cleveland administration might have done had it faced the same crisis. "I confess [that] some expressions of his letter stagger me and, if they bear the interpretation the President has put on them, and mean that Spain has been tricking us as regards autonomy and other matters incidental to it, I should have wanted the privilege of sending him his passports before he had any chance to be recalled or resign." [11] Few remarks better illustrated the continuity between Cleveland's and McKinley's diplo-

---

[11] McKinley's undated memorandum on the expected apology is in the Day papers, Cleveland, Ohio. Olney's remarks are contained in Olney to Cleveland, February 19, 1898, copy in Olney papers, Massachusetts Historical Society, Boston (abbreviated MHS hereafter).

macy, or the likelihood that, given the same events, war would have come in 1898 if the Democrat rather than the Republican had occupied the White House.

In Madrid Woodford was busy. Like McKinley he knew that speed was vital now as never before. If the home government delayed its apology it would seem to endorse de Lome's remarks. But speed was still alien to the Spanish. Latin politeness greeted the rapid step with which Woodford approached the Foreign Ministry. De Lome's resignation was already a fact, he was told blandly, and a new Minister was on his way. Woodford bluntly asked for a formal apology and remarked that it must come quickly to mollify American public opinion. The Foreign Minister was noncommittal; Spanish public opinion would condemn haste. Woodford left, but cabled home that negotiations on a trade treaty with Spain, to which de Lome had so offhandedly referred, should be hurried. Victory there would strengthen his hands in dealing over Cuba.

On February 14 Woodford again demanded an apology from the recalcitrant Spanish. When all else seemed to fail, he remarked angrily that he would resign if the apology were not forthcoming; he could hardly remain accredited to a country that slandered his chief of state. The Spanish assured him that an apology was ready, but in his private thoughts Woodford wondered if his abrupt tone had been wise. "With your generous and forgiving nature, you may think that I was possibly too positive and probably too severe," he cabled McKinley; "but I know that my decision is right, due alike to the affection I bear you and to my duty to our country."[12]

Finally, on February 16 Woodford received the Spanish apology, and despite its insolent tone, McKinley was willing to close the incident. "If a rupture between the two countries must come, it should not be upon any such personal and comparatively unimportant matter," Day cabled early in March as the affair's last ramifications settled.[13]

---

[12] Woodford to McKinley, February 15, 1898, Vol. 131A, Dispatches from Spain, RG 59, NA.

[13] Woodford to Sherman, February 17, 1898, *For. Rels., 1898*, 1012 ff; Day to Woodford, February 18, March 3, 1898, *ibid.*, 680–681.

McKinley might well have wished to end the vexing incident, for a week after the letter's publication a far greater tragedy occurred. The fall of 1897 had brought cooler weather to Cuba, and though anti-American tension seemed to subside, Lee was still anxious to have an American warship at his disposal in case of revolution or riots. By early January the President agreed that protection was necessary, and wished to combine this with an expression of friendliness. Day informed de Lome early in that month that the President wanted to resume friendly naval visits as a sign of lessening tension between the two countries. The U. S. S. *Maine,* one of the Navy's relatively new second-class battleships, would call in Havana harbor and Spanish ships would be welcome at an American port. Though some later students read sinister meaning into the visit, the administration intended none.

For a brief moment Lee thought the visit might increase tension and give false hope to the rebels. But when the *Maine* sailed into Havana harbor, "a beautiful sight and one long to be remembered," the Consul-General reported that the ship "has greatly relieved by her presence the Americans here."[14] The Spanish were cordial and polite in receiving the vessel, anxious to show every courtesy. But the ship symbolized American diplomatic pressure.

In Havana sailors from both fleets mingled casually, and many townspeople came down to the docks to see the ship and greet the American crew. The air was clean and warm, and the sailors' forays into the city brought the usual hauls of souvenirs. Everyone seemed gratified at the apparent hospitality. The days drifted past, punctuated by nothing more exciting than ship's drills. In the evenings Captain Sigsbee, the *Maine's* commander, wrote dispatches in his cabin. But on the evening of February 15, the ship shuddered in a massive explosion, and sank. Dawn revealed that nearly all the crew had perished in the disaster.

In Washington McKinley had retired early, exhausted from a day's worries and conferences. In the early morning hours, a watchman aroused him, and he listened on the telephone in a slight daze as Navy Secretary Long repeated information from

---

[14] Lee to Day, January 15, 26, February 5, 1898, Dispatches from Havana, RG 59, NA.

Lee in Havana. Trying to remain calm, the President hastily dressed and summoned officials for a long day's work.

The Spanish *chargé d'affaires* was also aroused, and he clattered to the State Department behind a frantic team to deliver his personal condolences and gain information. The officials he met were silent and wary, not having absorbed the tragedy's full import; but as he descended the steps half an hour later, he thought the Americans seemed to feel the explosion was an accident.

As dawn broke and the American people awoke, the newspaper headlines fairly rushing toward them, McKinley summoned his cabinet and congressional leaders. Hurrying toward the White House, they sensed that the long Cuban problem was now drawing to a close. To his old friend Representative Nelson Dingley of Maine, the President extended a hand of friendship. Dingley had never seen him look so worried. Lack of sleep, worry, and the tragedy itself had put dark rings around his eyes and a pallor on his face. His voice trembled slightly as he said that there must be no war because "the country was not ready for war."[15]

That day's cables brought distressing news to the impatient and edgy conferees in Washington. The ship was lost, few bodies had been recovered, and no one knew the explosion's cause. Tension was naturally high, but the Spanish were helping generously. As McKinley surveyed the field, his hopes sank. Only a month before he had told de Lome that they had every prospect for peace; now that Minister's letter and this fresh disaster unified his opponents and divided his friends. In his heart the President knew that intervention was but a matter of time. To Long he seemed aged and tired, "more oppressed and careworn than at any time since I have been in the Cabinet."[16]

As the public devoured news reports, and the yellow press rushed lurid extras to the streets, congressional tempers flared. Lodge would only say that "it is too serious to talk about at present." But Illinois' Republican Senator Shelby Cullom expressed a more blunt and widespread feeling. "I am too mad to talk about

---

[15] Edward Dingley, *Life and Times of Nelson Dingley, Jr.* (Kalamazoo, Mich.: Ihling and Everard, 1902), 454.

[16] Lawrence Shaw Mayo (Ed.), *America of Yesterday: As Reflected in the Journal of John Davis Long* (Boston: Atlantic Monthly Press, 1923), 165.

it. I can't see how the explosion could have been the result of an accident and I think the time is rapidly approaching when this country should do something." In the House, Reed and Dingley fought their way past angry members of both parties. The French ambassador reported home that "a sort of bellicose fury has seized the American people." And the Spanish *chargé* warned his government of something more alarming than the hot flash of public temper: "But aside from the belligerent feeling, I observe in the Administration a certain apprehension." Ex-Secretary of State Richard Olney summed up the month's events: "The Dupuy [de Lome] episode and the Havana explosion have furnished more material for the inflammation of popular passion against Spain than all that has happened during the last three years."[17] Once again he reflected the opinion that might have prevailed if Cleveland had been president.

McKinley's cabinet and military advisers were divided on the disaster's cause. Lee and Captain Sigsbee urged a suspension of popular feeling, and were willing for the moment to think that the explosion was accidental. The President himself felt, or perhaps hoped, that an investigation would prove this theory right. He tried to mollify angry congressmen and pursued his customary patient silence. He was still not eager for conflict, knowing its horrors from personal experience in the Civil War.

This seemed the logical time to break his long silence. Now seemed the crisis hour to use whatever moderate strength remained to support him, and to repudiate the jingoes publicly. But he held his silence, still fearing to feed prowar sentiment by speaking out. History has not understood or forgiven this reticence. His careful refusal to conduct public diplomacy or further confuse the Cuban issue by public pronouncements was an honest and understandable effort to stand above faction and function without entanglement in debate. But in the weeks that followed the de Lome letter, this silence worked against him. Both the public and history thought him confused and weak, but he had now begun to abandon his belief in negotiation. He did go to Philadelphia late in the month to tell an enormous crowd at the Uni-

---

[17] See Washington *Post*, February 16–18, 1898; Ernest R. May, *Imperial Democracy* (New York: Harcourt, Brace and World, 1961), 143; *Sp. Corr.*, 88; Olney to Cleveland, February 19, 1898, copy in Olney papers, MHS.

versity of Pennsylvania to suspend judgment until the Navy report was finished. "Such judgment, my fellow citizens, is the best safeguard in the calm of tranquil events, and rises superior and triumphant above the storm of woe and peril."[18] It sounded typical and it made sense to reasonable men, but slack applause greeted it.

Realizing at once that an official investigation was necessary, McKinley had quickly appointed a formal commission. With a presidential injunction to withhold nothing from their report and to be thorough within their competence, the Navy officers departed for Havana with divers and armor experts to examine the wrecked ship. The President rejected Spain's desire for a joint investigation. Public opinion would never countenance such cooperation, and, more importantly, a divided report would further inflame the situation.

Congressional opinion chafed, though most Americans awaited the official report. Almost everyone seemed convinced that it would merely confirm the general belief in Spanish guilt, a danger which diplomats saw only too clearly. The Spanish *chargé* warned his government: "All await with feverish anxiety the American official report. If it declares that the catastrophe was due to an accident, I believe I can assure your excellency that the present danger will be over; but if, on the contrary, it alleges that it was the work of a criminal hand, then we shall have to face the gravest situation."[19]

Madrid had hardly digested this warning before Day cabled Woodford a strong note on March 3. Seizing the opportunity to leave no mistake in Spanish minds about American purposes, and to capitalize on the tension, McKinley turned the diplomatic screw once again:

The de Lome incident, the destruction of the *Maine*, have added much to the popular feeling upon this subject [Cuba], although the better sentiment seems to be awaiting the report of the facts, and to follow the action of the President after the naval board has made its report. Whatever that report may be, it by no means relieves the situation

---

[18] *Speeches and Addresses of William McKinley* . . . (New York: Doubleday and McClure, 1900), 77.

[19] *Sp. Corr.*, 88.

of its difficulties. The policy of starvation, the failure of Spain to take effective measures to suppress the insurrection, the loss of our commerce, the great expense of patrolling our coast—these things, intensified by the insulting and insincere character of the de Lome letter, all combine to create a condition that is very grave, and which will require the highest wisdom and greatest prudence on both sides to avoid a crisis.[20]

The anti-autonomy riots in Havana of January 1898, the de Lome letter, and the *Maine* incident subtly but effectively turned American demands from Cuban autonomy to independence. It was now obvious to the administration that autonomy could not be instituted, and that it was not acceptable either to the Cubans or the American people. Spain must guarantee the final liberation of Cuba. The McKinley administration's historical reputation suffered for the lack of clarity around this change in demands. But Spain understood the new policy, which was clarified on the war's eve. She continued to assume before the world, however, that autonomy could be implemented and would satisfy American demands. It was a false view, but it gave her the best of the historical argument.

To emphasize the stiffening American attitude, McKinley called Illinois' crusty Republican Representative Joseph G. "Uncle Joe" Cannon to the White House for a conference. He spoke briefly and sincerely with the powerful Cannon, outlining with many gestures of the hands, as he paced up and down the room, just what he thought Congress should do. He wanted both houses to be patient and not force his hand, but he also wanted patriotic support. He still did not think war was necessarily inevitable, but if it should come, the country ought to be better prepared. He sat down and wrote out on a piece of paper the title of a bill appropriating fifty million dollars for defense, to be used at his discretion. He handed the paper to Cannon. This would show the Spanish he meant business, and would pacify a good deal of American opinion. It would also give Congress something positive to do. He hoped it would be a bipartisan measure; it would be wise not to exclude the Democrats in case of either war or peace. Cannon spent the afternoon and evening conferring with colleagues. On

---

[20] *For. Rels., 1898,* 680–681.

March 9 the bill was law, passed to thunderous applause in the press and the courts of public and congressional opinion.

It shocked the Spanish. "It has not excited the Spaniards, it has simply stunned them," Woodford cabled. "To appropriate fifty millions out of money in the treasury, without borrowing a cent, demonstrates wealth and power. Even Spain can see this. To put the money without restrictions at your disposal demonstrates entire confidence in you by all parties. The Ministry and press are simply stunned."[21] And yet the air of unreality that always surrounded Woodford's mission was still there. If the President desired peace, and hoped for prolonged negotiations, it was a strange time to ask for armaments. If he had gone over to the interventionists, further diplomacy was pointless. McKinley walked a fine line between the two, depending on just the right amount of pressure toward both to have his way. Woodford assumed that Congress still sustained the President, not stopping to think that all parties could vote for "national defense" without a twinge of conscience. From this time forward the administration had no alternative to intervention but complete Spanish capitulation to its demands. This was now the President's goal.

In the midst of all the confusion, the new Spanish Minister arrived, and upon presenting his credentials spoke of the prospects of peace. Even the aged Secretary Sherman shook his head in disbelief. It seemed to most policy makers that the Spanish still had no idea of the pressures working against peace. If the new Minister was at first innocent, however, he learned quickly. McKinley read him a little speech upon receiving his credentials which contained no surprise. "I have just been received by the President of the Republic, who made a most gracious address," Polo de Bernabe cabled home. "I fear, nevertheless, that the acts will not bear out the words."[22]

He was right, and support for his view came from many quarters. While McKinley made his last efforts for peace, Vermont's Republican Senator Redfield Proctor reported to the upper house on a recent tour of Cuba in toneless words and phrases that never-

---

[21] Woodford to McKinley, March 9, 1898, Vol. 131A, Dispatches from Spain, RG 59, NA.

[22] *Sp. Corr.*, 91.

theless set that body ablaze. On March 17 he spoke for several hours, giving a dispassionate review of his tour, reciting the horrors of reconcentration and economic prostration he had seen in Cuba. He concluded that Spain had neither the intent nor the power to reform the island.

The Senate was stunned. Accustomed to intemperate speeches on Cuba, it had awaited Proctor's report without enthusiasm. Instead of fiery phrases, he spoke calmly, almost coldly, of the horrors he saw. He shook both conservatives and moderates. "It is just as if Proctor had held up his right hand and sworn to it," said Maine's Republican Senator William P. Frye. Proctor's recent visit to the White House lent credence to the belief that if he did not speak for McKinley, the President at least had known the contents of the speech. Commercial papers reported that business circles received the speech favorably, and that last stronghold of support for the peace policy seemed to be slipping into the interventionist camp. Once again, the Spanish Minister reported uneasily. "Senator Proctor yesterday made a speech which has produced great effect because of its temperate stand. . . . My impression is that the President will try to withstand the powerful public sentiment in favor of the insurrection, but any incident might hinder his purposes."[23]

Public attention now turned to the elaborate report which the investigating commission was ready to send the President. The Spanish commission investigating the wrecked *Maine* reported that an internal accident destroyed the vessel, but American public opinion was in no mood to listen. The American court of inquiry reported that an external explosion sank the ship, assigning no blame. Most Americans would immediately assume that Spanish agents had planted a mine, without realizing that of all people involved, the Spanish had least to gain from such an incident.

While the country waited impatiently for the report and further action, Woodford stayed faithfully at his post. He conferred and argued with the Spanish officials, but to little avail. "They

---

[23] New York *Times*, March 18–25, 1898; Arthur Wallace Dunn, *From Harrison to Harding*, 2 vols. (New York: Putnam, 1922), I, 234; *Wall Street Journal*, March 19, 1898; *Sp. Corr.*, 93.

prefer the chance of war, with the certain loss of Cuba, to the overthrow of the dynasty."[24] On February 28 he reported that the Cortes had adjourned to lessen tension, but also perhaps to compound delay. By April the rainy season would begin in Cuba, and the Spanish could smilingly invoke the old seasonal argument to explain their lack of success in pacification. Day informed him on March 1 that American patience was almost ended. A day later the President himself again assured Woodford that Lee would not be removed from Havana.

As the tension mounted in both capitols, Woodford finally admitted that hope of speedy action was illusory. He suggested that Washington insist bluntly on Spanish haste to show that "the United States means business and means it *now*. The Spanish mind is so ingrained with 'mananaism' that few Spaniards ever act until they have to act." Washington answered late in March, saying bluntly that the *Maine* incident could be arbitrated, as the Spanish had proposed; but "the general condition of affairs in Cuba" could not be tolerated any longer. The President finally set a deadline; April 15 would be "none too early for accomplishment of these purposes." He added an appendix that jolted Woodford: "It is proper that you should know that unless events otherwise indicate, the President having exhausted diplomatic agencies to secure peace in Cuba will lay the whole matter before Congress."[25] Surely even the Spanish could see that meant war.

In the last days of March, McKinley entertained a long series of congressmen of all political persuasions, buying time and support from everyone he could impress. The pressure was such that he reluctantly agreed to send the relevant documents concerning Cuba to Congress if Spain did not act quickly. It was a last resort, which was not finally necessary.

Even McKinley's most optimistic friends and advisors now began to lose heart. "It was manifest that the loss of the *Maine* would lead to war, even if it were shown that Spain was innocent of her destruction," Secretary Long remembered. Senator Lodge noted with greater prescience: "If it is found that the *Maine* was

---

[24] *For. Rels., 1898,* 664–665.
[25] Woodford to McKinley, March 17, Day to Woodford, March 20, 1898, *ibid.,* 685–694.

blown up from the outside, it will be difficult to restrain the American people."[26] To the newspapers, discussion over guilt was academic. "Nine out of every ten American citizens doubtless believe firmly that the explosion which destroyed the *Maine* was the result of the cowardly Spanish conspiracy, and the Report of the Court of Inquiry will not tend to destroy that belief," trumpeted the Cleveland *Leader* on March 27. The Hearst press was even more rabid than usual, reveling in its own slogan: "Remember the *Maine* and to hell with Spain!"

For the first time the President was the target of violent public abuse. The widespread belief in his diplomacy and ability now began to crack. In Virginia a raging mob burned twin effigies of him and Hanna. McKinley's picture was hissed in theaters and torn from walls in some cities. Visitors to the Capitol saw jingoes sitting in the House and Senate galleries wrapped in American flags, and ladies who urged on their favorite demagogues with roses and smiles.

On March 25 McKinley received the commission's report and closeted himself with his advisors and Navy officers as they pored over complicated charts and diagrams. They ate lunch while working. It would be interesting to know what the experts privately told the President. Though they publicly assigned no guilt, they insisted firmly that an external explosion sank the *Maine*. Did they intend to imply that the Spanish set the torpedo? That idea filtered through press speculation and even into the President's war message of April 11, 1898, when he noted: ". . . the destruction of the *Maine*, by whatever exterior cause, is a patent and impressive proof of a state of things in Cuba that is intolerable." McKinley thought about the report over the weekend and then sent it and a message to Congress the following Monday.

The impatient congressmen were incredulous. It was the same story they had heard from McKinley for a year. His request for "deliberate consideration" and his whole patient and stubborn tone infuriated many members. On February 27 the Chicago *Tribune* had snapped editorially: "The people want no disgrace-

---

[26] John D. Long, *The New American Navy*, 2 vols. (New York: Outlook, 1903), I, 141; Lodge to Mr. Wright, February 28, 1898, Lodge papers, MHS.

ful negotiations with Spain. Should the President plunge his administration into that morass, he and his party would be swept out of power in 1900 by a fine burst of popular indignation. An administration which stains the national honor will never be forgiven." A closer reading showed that McKinley's message breathed a sense of the inevitable. Though he did not say that Spain's agents wrecked the ship, he argued subtly that the Spanish presence in Cuba created the conditions that indirectly destroyed the vessel by making her visit necessary.

That tone now flavored all dispatches that went to Spain. As experts studied the commission's report, Day cabled Woodford the President's last and most comprehensive plan, worked out in negotiation with congressional leaders and administration advisors. "A feeling of deliberation prevails in both houses of Congress," Day told Woodford, stretching the truth for diplomacy's sake, and outlined McKinley's plan: (1) Spain must freely grant an armistice to last until October, both sides to accept McKinley's good offices. (2) Spain would end reconcentration forever and undertake massive relief in Cuba. (3) If peace terms were not reached by October 1, McKinley would settle the Cuban problem as arbitrator. (4) If necessary, the President would approach the Cuban rebels directly for their participation in the plan if Spain first agreed. Implicit but not spelled out was the administration's central demand: Cuba must ultimately be independent. A mere cease-fire or suspension of hostilities would not be enough. The whole plan depended on speed.[27]

This was an act of virtual desperation for McKinley, since the plan contained nothing new, except its half-stated insistence on Cuban independence; and Spain had refused to permit American intervention since the days of Grant and Fish. She could never reform the island by October 1, except by granting independence; at no time had she even entertained such an idea. The President probably knew this, but wished to make one last comprehensive effort for the sake of conscience and the historical record.

Both Woodford in Madrid and his superiors in Washington feared congressional opinion. Only a dramatic breakthrough in negotiations would satisfy either or both houses. As congressmen

---

[27] For. Rels., 1898, 721–722.

of both parties looked at Cuban intervention, its virtues grew. To the Democrats it would end the frustrations of domestic defeat with foreign victory. To the wavering Republicans it would remove the explosive issue from politics and save them from the steamroller of public clamor. To each party it seemed a unifying issue that would help win future elections. "I trust we shall escape without a war," Lodge wrote with tongue in cheek, "but if we should have war we will not hear much of the currency question in the elections."[28] Congress always thought less of Spanish power than did the President. Senator Chandler snapped that any war with Spain would last between fifteen minutes and ninety days.

McKinley was certainly alive to the politics of the problem. He had already stretched his painfully built Republican coalition to the limit. If he resisted further, he might destroy his party and torpedo any future program of national development and international diplomacy. Though he did not say it, he knew of the feeling Senator Chandler expressed: "If [peace negotiations] had been prolonged the Republican party would have been divided, the Democrats would have been united, nothing would have been done and our party would have been overwhelmed in November."[29] It was pointless to quote Grover Cleveland to the effect that Congress might declare war but only the president could fight. If Congress declared war, what president would refuse to fight? Ugly scenes occurred at the White House and the State Department. An angry, cane-waving senator stormed into Day's office and pounded on the table. "By ———!" he yelled, "Don't your president know where the war-declaring power is lodged? Well tell him, by ———! that if he doesn't do something Congress will exercise the power and declare war in spite of him! He'll get run over and the party with him!"[30] Would Congress have done so? It is history's question. The administration's lines were not quite broken; McKinley could rally Aldrich, Platt, Hanna, and other stalwarts. But what would it profit him if he fragmented the party in doing so?

---

[28] Lodge to Henry [?], March 7, 1898, Lodge papers, MHS.
[29] Chandler to J. B. Foraker, October 15, 1898, Foraker papers, Historical and Philosophical Society of Ohio, Cincinnati.
[30] Jennie Hobart, *Memories* (Paterson, N. J.: privately printed, 1930), 61.

There was infinite irony in reflecting that McKinley, among the most peace-loving of men, might be remembered chiefly as a war president. How bitter he must have felt at reflecting what had become of his hopeful beginning. And he also remembered something almost pathetic that Woodford once said in a dispatch from Madrid: ". . . you, as a soldier, know what war is, even when waged for the holiest of causes."[31] The strain on him was obvious. His sleepless nights, long, hectic days, and endless worries cost him temper, nerves, and even affected his physical appearance.

Whatever his personal feelings, the processes of diplomacy now carried the President to the inevitable end. The last week of March brought a Spanish answer to American demands: yes, they would reform Cuba; yes, they would relieve reconcentration; yes, they would grant a cease-fire, but only if the rebels asked first; no, they would not accept presidential mediation. Woodford reported that the cabinet would confer on March 31, presumably to make a comprehensive reply to the President's demands. The message, which trickled over the cables in the small hours of March 31 and April 1, was not promising. Spain offered to arbitrate the *Maine* incident; to undertake relief; to accept American relief assistance; and to turn the Cuban problem over to the insular parliament, which would meet in Havana in May. But she would not accept mediation; there was no hint of granting Cuban independence. Woodford's disappointment shone through his dispatch. This was "the ultimate limit to which [Spain] can go in the way of concessions," but it was not enough. It did not immediately end reconcentration; promised only further delay on autonomy in a wrangling parliament; and was couched in such insulting tones that Long thought it ended McKinley's peace policy.[32]

Facing the critical likelihood of war, Spain still showed the unreality, confusion, and cross-purposes that always characterized her Cuban policy. Officials in the Colonial Office and even some men around Premier Sagasta admitted that Cuba was lost. They only wished to lose her in an honorable, face-saving manner. But Spanish domestic politics, national pride, and insular

---

[31] *For. Rels., 1898*, 685 ff.

[32] *Sp. Corr.*, 107–108; Long, *America of Yesterday*, 165.

interests in Cuba forbade such a negotiated settlement. Court circles, conservative politicians, and jingoistic nationalists preferred honorable defeat in war to any surrender to American demands. Woodford was told that Maria Christina herself had said bluntly "that she wished to hand over his patrimony unimpaired to her son when he should reach his majority; and that she would prefer to abdicate her regency and return to her Austrian home rather than be the instrument of ceding or parting with any of Spain's colonies." Though a desire to end the Cuban problem peacefully had finally penetrated a small number of Spanish officials, no significant Spanish policy makers ever considered acceding to American demands. There was simply no way for a Spanish government to solve the problem peacefully and remain in power or have any political future. "They know that Cuba is lost," Woodford cabled home, but he feared the ministry would seek honorable defeat in war.[33]

On April 4 Day delivered the expected answer which showed that American intervention was inevitable, barring total Spanish surrender:

We have received today from the Spanish Ministry a copy of the Manifesto of the Autonomy Government. It is not armistice. It proves to be an appeal by the Autonomy Government of Cuba urging the insurgents to lay down their arms and to join with the autonomy party in building up the new schemes of home rule. It is simply an invitation to the insurgents to submit, in which event the autonomy government, likewise suspending hostilities, is prepared to consider what expansion, if any, of the decreed home-rule scheme is necessary or practicable. It need scarcely be pointed out that this is a very different thing from an offered armistice.

Woodford could only ask for time, with the familiar suggestion that he might work out something.[34]

McKinley had no more time, and no more hope for a negotiated settlement. He set April 6 as the date his war message would go

---

[33] The Queen's remarks were repeated to Woodford by an official from the Colonial Office; see *For. Rels.*, *1898*, 693. Woodford's own views are in Woodford to McKinley, March 31, April 1, 1898, Dispatches from Spain, RG 59, NA.

[34] *For. Rels.*, *1898*, 733.

to Congress, but expectant crowds at the Capitol that day left disappointed. The President delayed until Lee evacuated American citizens in Cuba. Angry congressmen who crowded into his office demanding war met a rare show of presidential wrath. Calling his secretary, McKinley ordered the message locked in the White House safe until he was ready to send it.

On April 6 Woodford reported that the Spanish would consider papal intervention, and begged for a short delay. On that same day the ministers of the Great Powers arrived in McKinley's office to make a last gesture toward averting war. The President received the formal delegation in the Blue Room, gratefully noting Sir Julian Pauncefote, dean of the diplomatic corps, who represented an England widely known to favor American policies. Spain had conducted a long and complicated search for support among her continental neighbors, but despite anti-Americanism at some courts, no power was willing to act directly against either English or American interests. When the august delegation read its little speech deploring the coming conflict, McKinley tactfully read one of his own. They listened attentively and then withdrew. The New York *World* parodied the scene the next day. "We hope for humanity's sake you will not go to war," said the diplomats. "We hope if we go to war you will understand that it is for humanity's sake," McKinley replied.

Then the cables brought what appeared to be a fresh break on April 9: Spain would suspend hostilities in Cuba and extend the promises of reform, acting on the advice of the pope. Did it change anything? "I hope that nothing will now be done to humiliate Spain," Woodford urged in an accompanying dispatch, "as I am satisfied that the present Government is going and is loyally going to go as fast and as far as it can. With your power of action sufficiently free you will win the fight on your own lines."[35] A quick talk with Lodge, Senator Aldrich, and others convinced McKinley that the answer was not sufficient. Events had passed them all by; it seemed doubtful now that such an armistice could be enforced. It would only prolong an intolerable situation. McKinley appended the last Spanish note to his war message

---

[35] See Woodford to Day, April 8, 9, 1898, Day papers; Washington *Post*, April 11, 1898; *For. Rels., 1898,* 747.

and transmitted both to Congress on April 11, making it clear
that he no longer believed in Spain's ability to end the Cuban
problem peacefully:

The long trial has proved that the object for which Spain has waged
the war cannot be attained. The fire of insurrection may flame or
may smolder with varying seasons, but it has not been and it is
plain that it cannot be extinguished by present methods. The only
hope of relief and repose from a condition which can no longer be
endured is the enforced pacification of Cuba. In the name of humanity, in the name of civilization, in behalf of endangered American
interests which give us the right and the duty to speak and to act,
the war in Cuba must stop.

And so it ended. Some said he should have accepted the final
Spanish offer, since it surrendered to American demands. But it
was a specious "surrender." It spurned American mediation or
control of the process of suspending hostilities. It offered no
genuine or enforceable program either to pacify Cuba or grant
the island autonomy. It said nothing of ultimate Cuban independence, now the basic American demand. When Day asked the
Spanish Minister if these last-minute concessions implied ultimate Cuban independence, he answered with a single word:
"No."[36] To assume that this cease-fire promised a peaceful long-
term settlement was an act of faith which nothing in Spain's past
diplomacy or present capabilities warranted. The measure of its
hollowness lay in the failure even of McKinley's opponents to
take it seriously. No substantial element of the press or Congress
suggested that it marked a path to peace. The President no longer
believed that Spain could carry out any promises she made. No
historical evidence shows that he was wrong. Only two solutions
were now possible: the war might continue indefinitely in Cuba,
or the United States could intervene and expel Spain, reform
the island, and end the issue once and for all. There was no middle
ground. If McKinley delayed, his party would be defeated in the
November elections. With jingoes packing both houses, an
aroused press, and a people favoring war, conflict would come.
But that entered into the President's thinking less than the final

---

[36] See May, *Imperial Democracy*, 157.

realization that the ideas he had hoped to implement peacefully could now be achieved only by force.[37]

What went wrong? What ruined the President's painfully pursued hope of a peaceful settlement? The real fault in McKinley's diplomacy was not a lack of consistency or courage, but of imagination and alternatives. He sought peace by the only means available, threatening war, and continued Cleveland's policy of pressuring Spain, gambling that she would give way rather than face a war she could only lose. The basic problem was a lack of alternatives to intervention.

How easy it is to argue with all the textbooks that an addition to the President's spine would have averted the conflict, or that had Cleveland been president there would have been no war. The diplomacy of the two men was similar, but the conditions in which they worked greatly differed. Cleveland did not face the de Lome letter, the *Maine* incident, or the failure of autonomy; nor was the Cuban issue ablaze in the press and Congress as much as under McKinley.

McKinley's methods differed from Cleveland's, for he was more flexible in his approach and more responsible to his critics and supporters alike. But he did not "surrender" to public opinion. He merely accepted as inevitable what he had feared all along; intervention was necessary to free Cuba and to attain America's diplomatic and economic goals in the hemisphere. The chief personal weakness of his diplomacy was his silence. Fearful of being misunderstood or inflaming the issue, he remained silent during the whole long crisis. Had he defined his position publicly in 1897, and certainly in the great crises of 1898, he might have rallied some added public opinion to his side. He could not have prevented the war, but he could have clarified and justified his own record.

---

[37] Two years later when he was a federal judge, Day looked back on these events with some misgivings about how history would judge McKinley. He asked John Bassett Moore to write a history of the conflict, and urged strongly that "the diplomatic history of that period to be really intelligible, should be supplemented by an account of the condition of affairs in Cuba, the failure of the promised reforms, the lack of real self-government in the proposed autonomy, in short, the general failure of the Spanish promises and plans for the betterment of conditions in Cuba." Day to Moore, December 24, 1900, Moore papers, Library of Congress, Manuscripts Division, Washington, D. C.

A bolder and more vigorous mind might have cut through the
tedium of diplomacy with a striking idea to move ahead of both
the Spanish and the Cuban rebels. McKinley might have called
for an international meeting between his government and that of
Spain, at which a settlement could at least have been proposed.
But American public opinion would never have tolerated such a
summit conference. It would have created more problems than
it solved. What, for example, would be the Cubans' status at such
a conference? Would not both Spain and the United States insist
upon an agenda, consuming endless time, thus aiding Spain's policy of inaction? Could an award made at such a conference have
been justified to the people of Spain, Cuba, or the United States?
Probably not. In any event, McKinley was not the man to set such
a startling precedent in American diplomacy. He might have
served Spain with an ultimatum, but that would merely have ac-
celerated war's arrival. He might have quietly asked the Powers
to pressure Spain, but they were already more sympathetic to
her than the United States. American public opinion would never
have tolerated such an abandonment of freedom of action. He
might have called for an investigation in Cuba by an international
commission, its judgment to be final. But who involved would
have agreed to such a commission, much less accepted its find-
ings? All such suggestions seem unreal when set in their late nine-
teenth-century context.

What policy might have saved the peace? Inaction was impossible, and whatever McKinley did offended some strong body
of opinion. If he could have conducted his policy alone; if Spain
had been more amenable to rapid reform; if the Cubans had not
been so irksome and had no influence in Congress and the press;
if the American people had been more patient—the "ifs" mount
up, showing the bleakness of the President's task. The problem
was old, fraught with hidden complexities and unseen contin-
gencies. If there be blame for the war, it should rest fairly with
everyone concerned: the Spanish and Cubans, the American people and press, and the diplomatic policies of Cleveland and Mc-
Kinley.

McKinley thus accepted the responsibilities of intervening in
Cuba. Humanitarian desires to relieve the island's suffering, to
make it free, and to establish a Latin-American democracy were
uppermost in his own mind. Americans of a later generation will

understand these motives. But the administration and influential blocs of public opinion also wanted to eliminate Spain from the New World. Future American influence in the Caribbean and all of Latin America required a free Cuba. Strategic interest in a two-ocean Navy, and an isthmian canal unthreatened by a Spanish Cuba, figured in the minds of military and diplomatic planners. Rehabilitation of the Cuban economy and future trade with the island certainly moved many men.

But for the moment, all was anticlimax as a whooping Congress received the President's war message. On April 4 McKinley had read a draft to his cabinet and Long recorded his disappointment. The President's lack of rest, his worry, and fast-moving events combined to produce a lengthy and often halting document. The message astonished Congress, which had expected a bugle call for action. McKinley's firm refusal even now to recognize Cuban independence irritated many congressmen. He listed four basic reasons for intervention: (1) for humanity's sake and to end the devastation of Cuba, (2) to protect American citizens and rights in the island, (3) to end the dangers to both Cuban and American commerce, and (4) to guarantee American strategic rights in the hemisphere.

Many congressmn criticized the document as too conservative. "It is the weakest and most inconclusive speech sent out by any President," Texas Senator Joe Bailey snapped. "President's message on Cuba—disappointing," Chandler noted in his little red pocket diary. "I have no patience with the message and you may say so," Ohio Republican Joseph B. Foraker told a reporter. "I have heard nothing but condemnation of the message on all hands," remarked Senator Rawlins of Utah. "The message is weak, impotent, imbecile and disgraceful."[38]

During the debate that followed, a large bloc of senators favored recognizing Cuban independence, but the administration defeated the plan. The President wanted a free hand in dealing with Cuba during and after war; there would be time enough to prepare for her independence later. Senator Henry M. Teller of Colorado amended the war resolution to forbid American acquisi-

---

[38] Sam Acheson, *Joe Bailey* (New York: Macmillan, 1932), 105; Chandler Diary, April 11, 1898, New Hampshire Historical Society, Concord; Washington *Post*, April 12, 1898.

tion of the island. After much debate and rewording, the joint resolution reached the President's desk on April 20. The nation now closed ranks enthusiastically. When the President signed the ultimatum to Spain, the New York *Sun* trumpeted: "We are all jingoes now; and the head jingo is the Hon. William McKinley, the trusted and honored Chief Executive of the nation's will."

As the country prepared for war, Senator George F. Hoar, later head of an anti-expansionist Republican minority, wrote a letter vividly stating the ideas that compelled honest men to war:

I had hoped and expected that the mission of this country would be [that of] the great Peacemaker among nations, both by example and influence. But we cannot look idly on while hundreds of thousands of innocent human beings, women and children and old men, die of hunger close to our doors. If there is ever to be a war it should be to prevent such things as that. The demoralization which comes to a people from preventing such things cannot be greater than that which comes to them from permitting them. I shall do everything in my power to sustain the President so long as I can see a glimpse of hope for getting Spain out of Cuba by peaceful means. But I shall sustain him also if he finds it necessary to resort to force. If ever there should be a war it should be in such a cause. If guns and ships of war are ever to be used they are to be used on such an occasion.[39]

This was the feeling that brought war. This same feeling would make its results among the most bitter issues in recent American politics.

---

[39] Hoar to William Claflin, April 12, 1898, Claflin papers, Rutherford B. Hayes Memorial Library, Fremont, Ohio.

CHAPTER IV

The Splendid Little War

THE COUNTRY WENT TO WAR in a holiday mood that reflected its
ignorance of the realities of either combat or world responsibilities. Flags blossomed in the streets and along front verandas
in towns and cities, while martial music guided the way to re-
cruiting booths. Young men eagerly stood in line to volunteer,
joking and smiling, gathering a harvest of free drinks from men
and kisses from ladies. Many young American men were already
imbued with the desire to kill a Spaniard; the press and events
had done their work well.

In Washington the administration had a triple problem: to
raise and prepare an army, to direct a new diplomacy, and to
treat with foreign powers with whose interests they might clash.
Though most continental countries made no secret of their lik-
ing for Spain, none ventured to interfere. Americans took comfort from the knowledge that Great Britain supported their aims,
and her support helped warn most hostile foreign sentiment away.
In London the Union Jack and the Stars and Stripes flew from the
same pole. Ambassador Hay worked assiduously, as he did the
rest of his career, to make the unwritten understanding between
the two countries binding and real.

At home McKinley faced a small diplomatic crisis of his own;
Secretary Sherman retired on April 25, and the President quickly
chose Day as his temporary successor. In September John Hay
formally took the office, indicating a basic change in the administration's foreign policy. The appointment of such an experienced
man, whose intelligence, foreign travel, and friends fortified his
widely known internationalism, highlighted America's entry into
world politics.

Optimism was high but the conflict had its unpleasant side. Lodge's friends had called the Spanish harmless orange peddlers, but they did have a fleet; and intelligence being what it was in those days, the Navy did not really know how good it was. Rumor had Admiral Cervera, out of the Azores with a powerful squadron, within sight of New York, Providence, Boston, and Washington. Hysterical state governors and local defense committees envisioned shots falling in the streets of a hundred towns, as if the Spanish Navy covered the whole Atlantic. The American Navy knew better, but it was hard to calm public fears. There were minor inconveniences, some of which highlighted the war's whole nature. Society editors warned their readers not to open their summer cottages at Newport until the danger passed.

But these fears were scattered and unimportant, for the nation rallied to the flag with fervor. Helen Gould gave the government her yacht and a hundred thousand dollars. Wall Street's denizens organized a fighting unit, as if to atone for their recalcitrance in pushing for war. William Astor Chandler gave the government a regiment. From the west came a familiar voice: William Jennings Bryan offered his services for the cause. The President was not one to make an opponent a hero; and though "Colonel" Bryan headed a volunteer Nebraska regiment, he never got out of training camp in Florida, where, according to Mr. Dooley, he had plenty of time to preach his hellish doctrines to the alligators.

The Army which McKinley commanded, in time-honored American fashion, was wholly unprepared and pathetically small. Congressional penury, a long period of peace, and American distrust of professional armies and belief in the citizen soldier combined to give the country an army hardly large enough to police the remaining frontier or stage a good parade. There had not been a brigade formation in the Army since Reconstruction ended, and most officers had never seen more than a regiment of men even on maneuvers. Crucial services like ordnance, procurement, and training were all geared to this monumentally inadequate level.

When the war came, there were fifty-seven experts in the quartermaster corps ready to supply a raw army of 250,000 men. Most of the fifty million dollars appropriated in March wisely went to the Navy, always the country's first line of defense. Equipment was antiquated and irregular; uniforms issued varied so much in hue that a company looked like a rainbow. There were not enough rifles to train the volunteers; field guns and long-range artillery to support an invasion or assault were scarce and antiquated. Even the Spanish used smokeless powder, but the American Army still used black powder that revealed a field gun's position with each shot. Promotion was slow in all the services, and military thinking was even slower. Theodore Roosevelt remembered seeing first lieutenants with white beards lead their men into battle. One bewildered quartermaster summed up the confusion and pressure: "There were so many changes."[1]

The armed forces predictably descended into snarls of red tape and confusion as the call to arms sounded. Howls of protest condemned the services for their ineptitude. Why was the country so ill-prepared, when the crisis had loomed for years? It was easy to blame the administration in general, and Secretary of War Alger in particular. But though neither was blameless, their problems were understandable. A generation of neglect had rusted not only equipment but men; the inertia of the system made it almost impossible to change without a revolution in thought. The President could hardly have prepared for war while seeking peace. Mobilization was cumbersome and slow. He could not have rallied the nation in a show of force or modernized the services prior to April 1898 without ending the hope of a peaceful settlement. The mere process of calling up reservists from the states, of seeking money from Congress, of revamping the command system would have ended McKinley's tenuous influence in Congress and the press. It would also have been a kind of ultimatum to Spain that would merely have brought war sooner. The naval appropriation of March 1898 was the best McKinley could do without completely abandoning negotiations.

The country never thought itself weak, however confused its armed might seemed to foreign observers. Those who saw the first regulars march into training camps felt a little thrill. They were clean, bronzed, healthy-looking men, nucleus of the vast new volunteer army. Some of the regular units would be retained for invasion and shock cadres. On April 22 the President blockaded Cuba; on the following day he called for 125,000 volunteers.

---

[1] Walter Millis, *The Martial Spirit* (New York: Literary Guild of America, 1931), 214–215.

Before the war ended some 270,000 men entered the Army, though only part of them saw actual combat service. The administration wanted a regular Army of at least 100,000, with long-term enlistments. But Congress compromised on 60,000 regulars for two-year terms. State politicians, the national guard lobbies, and others who benefitted from the existing system were too powerful to resist until McKinley began to revamp the Army under a new Secretary, Elihu Root, after 1899.

How to make a fighting army from these raw and over-enthusiastic volunteers? As the Army crowded into hastily activated training camps, camping on the lawns of state capitols and courthouses, chafing to kill Spaniards, McKinley moved with his usual deliberation. It would hardly do to throw green troops against the Spanish and start with a defeat. There were the added problems of land and sea transportation, naval protection, equipment and supply, and favor seekers. These last, hardly a new factor to politicians, now redoubled their assaults on the White House, seeking military commissions and contracts. Senators and representatives offered the President their states' votes in return for contracts, slyly hinting that if he did not recognize them, their later support might be even more expensive. To his credit McKinley resisted such blandishments well. Having been a soldier himself, knowing the disastrous results of "political generals" in the Civil War, he did not wish to mar his own administration with incompetent, if politically sagacious, appointments. If nothing but Army expansion and reorganization came out of the war, it might be worth the cost. On the whole he did very well. Out of the 26 major generals he appointed, 19 were regulars; of the 102 brigadiers, 66 were regulars. In the administrative and supply posts so crucial to a modern army, he placed experienced men whenever he could find them. But even in June, with fighting at hand, his private secretary noted no abatement in favor-seeking. "All hands are still interested in Army appointments," he wrote drily.[2]

McKinley, however, was a noted politician; few men could accommodate so many disparate purposes at the same time. The

---

[2] See Arthur Wallace Dunn, *From Harrison to Harding*, 2 vols., (New York: Putnam, 1922), I, 241; Margaret Leech, *In The Days of McKinley* (New York: Harper, 1959), 236.

last Civil War veteran in the White House, he was especially anxious to use the conflict to erase sectional feeling. He could hardly overlook the South, always vociferous in its desire to free Cuba. Her "Confederate brigadiers" were anxious to wear blue again. The first logical choice was Georgia's aged "Fighting Joe" Wheeler, long an expansionist congressman who wanted to serve the old flag. The President greeted him with outstretched hands in May. "There must be a high ranking officer from the South," he said. "There must be a symbol that the old days are gone— you are needed." He did not have to beg; Wheeler took to the field and fought eagerly if not always wisely.[3]

As May passed and the army gradually formed, the war planners turned anxiously to the Navy. Transport was critical in mounting this first large-scale American amphibious operation. The government began buying and leasing steamers, yachts, transports, tonnage of any kind. It was hastily inspected, overhauled, and equipped with the necessary facilities for carrying men, animals, and the supplies they would need. Food was a special problem, since there were few prepared rations. The Armour Company promised a refrigerator ship, and the quartermaster corps momentarily prided itself on a recent acquisition of vast stores of canned beef.

But confusion, cross-purposes, and disorder were inevitable, and the country grew first impatient and then angry as it watched the War Department ensnarled in its own red tape. Eager for war, the public easily forgot that the nation never had an adequate armed force when crisis came. The very Congress that had done so much to start the war did precious little to prepare for it. To those in charge the confusion was doubly clear, though they were more likely to see that it was "no more than naturally follows the transition from a state of peace to a state of war in a country situated as ours is."[4]

---

[3] Charles S. Olcott, *Life of William McKinley*, 2 vols. (Boston: Houghton-Mifflin, 1916), II, 264; Charles Johnson Post, *The Little War of Private Post* (Boston: Little, Brown, 1960), 214–215.

[4] John J. McCook to James Wilson, June 4, 1898, Wilson papers, Library of Congress, Manuscripts Division, Washington, D. C. (abbreviated LC hereafter).

If matters were snarled at Washington, they were frightful at Tampa, chosen as the embarkation point for Cuba. Located in a fairly mild climate on Florida's west coast, the port boasted a harbor and proximity to the fighting zone. It had little else. A single track railway led over its sandy expanse to utterly inadequate piers, and the jumble of boxcars backed up for miles made supply a wilderness of problems. Food, water, and medicines were short; fodder for animals was rare. More than one regiment was assigned the same transport, and many commanders followed Theodore Roosevelt's example and simply seized what they needed.

At the war's other end, public anger focused on Secretary of War Russell Alger, late of Michigan. McKinley's judgment of men was usually exceptional, but in taking Alger into his cabinet for the sake of geography and politics, he made a serious blunder. Vain, waspishly touchy about his own power and prestige, sickly and craving power, the finicky Secretary and his age-encrusted bureau chiefs were natural whipping boys for public and official frustration. Congressmen like Senator Lodge frankly wanted Alger's scalp, and urged the President to make a clean sweep of the War Department, using the broom first at the top. McKinley would not sacrifice the hapless Secretary for another year, and was willing as usual to shoulder added burdens and help direct routine War Department affairs himself. He did tire of Alger's curious combination of bluster and delay. "I do remember that you had your war days and your anti-war days," McKinley once noted.[5] But even the strain of war did not kill McKinley's sense of humor. He followed both men and events closely. When the war was over, he asked a major, famous for having stolen another regiment's supplies, to do a difficult job. When the man demurred, the President spread his hands and smiled knowingly: "Charlie, any man who can steal the rations of a whole regiment can do anything."[6]

McKinley's immediate problems now centered on the men who would actually direct the fighting. There was no central staff system or planning agency. In the Army he encountered the im-

---

[5] See Vol. 34, n.d., McKinley papers, LC; apparently in answer to Alger's letter of December 28, 1899.
[6] Olcott, *William McKinley*, II, 366–367.

pressive figure of Major General Commanding, Nelson A. Miles. One of the last "boy generals" of the the Civil War, Miles earned a fabulous reputation as an Indian fighter and climbed the ladder of Army success until he had nowhere to go but the ornate and rather empty office he now filled. Married to John Sherman's niece, he had long criticized the administration, and it was no secret that the presidential bee had a nest in his bonnet. Even Theodore Roosevelt disliked "the brave peacock," for the General was overbearing and did not hide his likes and dislikes. In theory he supervised all military actions.

Field command fell by lot of seniority to an even more embarrassing figure, General William R. Shafter, who weighed over 250 pounds. Slow of movement, and cautious of mind and decision, he did not inspire vigor in his troops. Steeped in the routines of paper work and addicted to form, he seemed wholly illogical for a field command. But he was a brave and steady soldier, given more to life-saving deliberation than to rash assault. His corpulent, half-comical, half-pathetic figure, swathed in a tight uniform and crowned with a pith helmet, became a familiar figure to the men in Cuba. He rode along the lines in his celebrated sagging buckboard or perched solidly atop his diminutive yet persistent "stout-hearted mule," the subject of soldier songs and poetry.

The command situation was somewhat better in the Navy, for that branch of the service had prospered more than the Army. A decent fleet was part of national pride, and its reconstruction and conversion to modern steam vessels began under Chester Arthur, and was continued by every subsequent president. In the Atlantic the chilly but efficient William T. Sampson would command. In the Pacific the Navy would produce the war's greatest hero, Commodore and then Admiral George Dewey. In the fall of 1897 McKinley had approved Navy Department plans to station Dewey in Hong Kong, so that he might attack the Philippines when and if war came. Though he did not perhaps know that he was making a great war hero in the process, the President knew very well what he was doing in relation to the Orient long before war came. Though Long and Roosevelt wanted Dewey to strike in mid-April, McKinley delayed until war was official, and on April 24 the signal went to Hong Kong that took Dewey to his rendezvous with destiny.

On the night of April 30 Dewey's squadron passed through the straits that led to Manila's harbor. The channel was mined and the guns from the rock fortress of Corregidor were supposedly powerful; he did not know the exact strength or power of the Spanish fleet in Manila. But the guns and mines were either silent or ineffective, and on the morning of May 1 his ships stood opposite the Spanish squadron in Manila Bay.

In Washington, half a world away, the day was pleasant, carrying a trace of summer heat, but in Manila it was tropical. As Dewey's ships moved to battle, the engine rooms and gunners' turrets turned to ovens, and one sailor remarked laconically: "We people don't have to worry, for Hell ain't no hotter than this!"[7] The Spanish found the morning's work far hotter, and when the battle ended their fleet lay twisted in wreckage on the harbor bottom. Dewey cut the cable leading to Hong Kong to insure secrecy, for his ships attacked the fleet, not the Spanish garrison in Manila itself. On May 2 rumor from Madrid and other European capitals circulated in Washington, telling of a great naval battle; but the word was not official until May 7, when one of Dewey's ships reported from Hong Kong.

America went wild at the news. Action at last had come from the welter of confusion and delay surrounding the effort to free Cuba. Millions of hearts thrilled to the sounds of martial music, the sight of fireworks, and the thought of victory's meaning. A triumph of bad newspaper poetry summed up the feeling:

> Oh, dewy was the morning,
> Upon the first of May,
> And Dewey was the admiral,
> Down in Manila Bay.
> And dewy were the Spaniards' eyes.
> Them orbs of black and blue,
> And dew we feel discouraged?
> I dew not think we dew!

That victory came in another hemisphere and in a place of which most Americans had never heard did not matter. A hero was a hero, and Dewey was certainly the war's most compelling name.

---

[7] Millis, *The Martial Spirit*, 188.

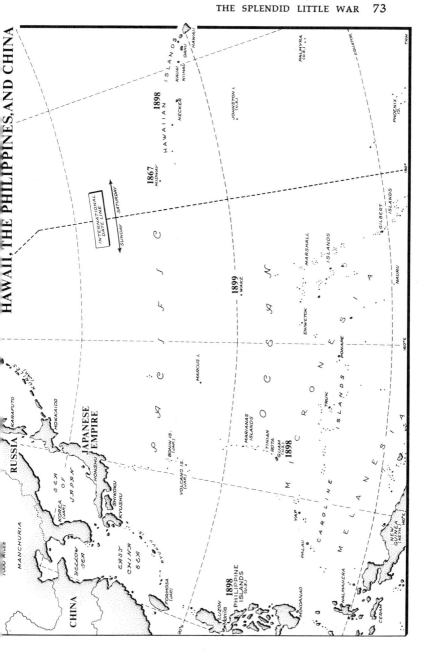

HAWAII, THE PHILIPPINES, AND CHINA

MORGAN MAP 2 W-2

McKinley, though hardly ignorant of either the battle or its consequences, was as ill-equipped as many subordinates, and at first followed action on a schoolbook map of the Orient. A member of the Coast and Geodetic Survey took him a detailed chart of the Philippines. After a half hour's talk, he bowed out his visitor with a remark applicable to many of his countrymen: "It is evident that I must learn a great deal of geography in this war. . . ."[8]

The very name "Philippines" drew a blank with most Americans, and Mr. Dooley later said he thought they were canned goods. But it did not really matter; the Stars and Stripes flew somewhere. On May 2, before Dewey's victory was confirmed, McKinley in conference with military and diplomatic advisors authorized a relief expedition to the islands. General Wesley Merritt was ordered to assault Manila with a force of regulars and volunteers, whose first contingent would shortly leave from San Francisco.

The battle was no sooner reported than Americans rushed to their maps. Then in a second breath many demanded retention of the islands as spoils of war and outposts of Oriental empire. Though cautious administration spokesmen held their tongues, the expansionist press began its long rallying cry. "Common sense tells us to keep what has cost so much to wrest from an unworthy foe," said a Baltimore paper. "Back of that is the solid, irresistible sentiment of the people."[9]

Suspicions of foreign powers and their designs in the Orient intensified this emerging demand for empire. Germany, France, Great Britain, Japan, and heaven knew who else had ships and agents in the Orient; if America did not take the Philippines, they would, many reasoned. This would be disastrous for American diplomacy and trade in the East. As usual, congressmen were more outspoken than men in the administration. "The fear I have about this war is that peace will be declared before we can get full occupation of the Philippines and Porto Rico," Senator

---

[8] Henry S. Pritchett, "Some Recollections of President McKinley and the Cuban Intervention," *North American Review*, 189 (March 1909), 397–403.

[9] Millis, *The Martial Spirit*, 181 ff; Baltimore *American*, June 11, 1898; New York *Tribune*, May 5, 1898; Cleveland *Plain Dealer*, May 5, 1898; Chicago *Inter-Ocean*, May 31, 1898.

Frye said bluntly.[10] Expansionist appetites everywhere sharpened under the impact of events. In the Navy, Mahan raised a powerful voice, influencing congressmen and diplomats as well as brother officers.

In the confusion of attitudes that followed during the summer, one newspaper plaintively asked: Why is Uncle Sam like a lady throwing a stone? Because he aimed at Cuba and hit the Philippines. And a great many Americans appreciated a newspaper rhymster's contribution:

> O Dewey at Manila
> That fateful first of May,
> When you sank the Spanish squadron
> In almost bloodless fray,
> And gave your name to deathless fame;
> O glorious Dewey, say,
> Why didn't you weigh anchor
> And softly sail away?

Opinion over retaining the islands was divided within the administration. As July closed and the President had said nothing beyond the usual generalities, those around him felt he was "conservative" on the issue. To one visitor, however, he showed clearly that he already favored overseas expansion. He wanted to retain as little as possible from the war's conquests, but he did not yet know how much that little would be. He thought that "the general principle of holding on to what we get" was wise. If events dictated, he would keep all the archipelago. Impressed by the President's words and his whole demeanor, his listener promptly assured Senator Lodge that McKinley was an expansionist.[11] From the very first, McKinley inclined toward retaining all the Philippines. He now deftly and circuitously began to develop public opinion to support his decision.

McKinley showed his sympathies with expansion by using the war emergency to annex Hawaii. He had always considered this a consummation of long-standing Republican policy, not an

---

[10] Frye to James Wilson, June 6, 1898, Wilson papers, LC.

[11] Charles G. Dawes, *A Journal of the McKinley Years* (Chicago: Lakeside Press, 1950), 166; W. M. Laffan to Lodge, July 14, 1898, Lodge papers, Massachusetts Historical Society, Boston.

innovation. He permitted the annexation treaty to languish until the war because he was unwilling to add it to his burdens in dealing with Cuba. Members of his own party opposed Hawaiian annexation. In the House, Speaker Reed showed members with a piece of string and a terrestrial globe that the distance from the United States to Asia was shorter via the already American-owned Aleutian Islands than through Hawaii. He convinced few, and missed the essential point; annexation was never of the head but of the heart. In July, using the war and its resulting need for naval bases in the Pacific, pointing out that Hawaii would be the major stepping stone to American penetration in the Orient, the administration pushed through a joint resolution annexing the islands, and the President signed it on July 7. By now resistance to the scheme was futile. Senator Hoar favored it, saying in justification for his divided stand on expansion that the Hawaiians welcomed American rule, while the Filipinos did not. The expansionists easily saw Hawaii's importance; it was a beginning, not an end. If it could be acquired, what would stop acquisition of the Philippines? "To maintain our flag in the Philippines, we must raise our flag in Hawaii," the New York *Sun* said candidly.[12]

The situation in the Philippines was much more complicated. The Filipinos welcomed Americans there as liberators, not as conquerors. Like the Cubans, they had long been in revolt against the Spanish, and claimed a George Washington in the person of Emilio Aguinaldo. Always jealous of his prerogatives, and claiming to head a genuinely popular Philippine Republic, Aguinaldo watched Dewey and his ships with suspicion. For the moment their guns only dominated the Spanish forts; but who could tell what the Americans would do after a land force arrived and they invaded the islands? The Filipinos and Americans were nervous allies.

Alive to the dangers involved, the State Department quickly forbade any diplomatic communication with or promise to the insurgents. Washington insisted that the islands were under American control alone until a peace treaty settled their fate. Though he worried over the "insurgent complication," as he called

---

[12] New York *Sun*, June 1, 1898.

it, the politically inept Dewey never really understood the problem. His wavering advice to officials at home further complicated
an already touchy problem. In June Aguinaldo ominously proclaimed his republic, with himself as president.

To counter this tension and to relieve Dewey, the first Army
contingent left San Francisco on May 25. Its commander brought
the President's instructions. McKinley said nothing of Philippine
independence, but promised cooperation and kindness; events
would formulate a firmer policy as soon as he had adequate information. He held out a slender, unspoken hope of self-rule. In
the meantime, "Our occupation should be as free from severity
as possible."[13]

The public at home found the Philippine situation too complicated to understand and much less pressing than the long-
awaited Cuban invasion. In late May and early June, attention
turned south to Florida, where the Army prepared to embark
helter-skelter for Cuba. General Miles sensibly wished to delay
any assault until the fall, when cooler weather and better training among his men, not to mention adequate equipment, would
cost fewer lives and create less difficulty. The President might
gladly have agreed, but the public was rabid for war.

In Tampa Shafter looked at his army with dismay. He frankly
did not know how they were to get to Cuba. By the first week
in June, McKinley's patience was exhausted, and he ordered the
Army to embark at once. Sampson's fleet had blockaded Santiago
de Cuba, and all seemed ready. The President's orders provoked
a mad rush to embark, and the men packed themselves, their
animals, and equipment into stifling ships' holds, eager to cast off.
There was an inevitable delay, however. Rumors that the Spanish
Atlantic squadron threatened the coast drew some of Sampson's
covering fleet from Cuba, and the men off Tampa roasted in their
ships for a week while the futile chase ensued.

On June 20 the invasion flotilla finally arrived off Cuba, and for
about a week disembarked in disorder at Siboney and Daiquiri.
Boats carrying reporters, who thought the invasion their private
theater made the confusion monumental. Happily, resistance was

---

[13] U.S. War Department, *Correspondence Relating to the War with Spain
. . .*, 2 vols. (Washington, 1902), II, 676–678.

nominal; and while supporting units rowed ashore, and experienced cavalrymen swam their horses to the beaches, the first contingents pushed along unknown trails into the interior. By month's end Shafter's Army was within a mile of Santiago, ready either to storm or lay siege. On July 1 and 2 San Juan Hill and its adjacent high territory were engraved on American military history, and the folks at home had a fresh supply of heroes and controversy over who did what. A gala naval victory followed as a Fourth of July present when Sampson and Commodore Winfield Scott Schley sank the Spanish fleet as it tried to escape from Santiago harbor.

Shafter now began to negotiate rather than to fight. Aware of his command's problems—poor supplies, bad communications, thin lines, and the threat of disease—he was anxious to avoid assaulting Santiago. He would fight if ordered, but warned the President to "be prepared for heavy losses among our troops."[14]

The President did not object to peace by the pen rather than the sword and authorized negotiations with the Spanish on the basis of unconditional surrender. The Spanish offered to leave the city without a fight if the Americans would allow them to keep their weapons and give them a day's march before attacking. McKinley sternly vetoed this absurd scheme. "What you went to Santiago for was the Spanish army," he cabled. "If you allow it to evacuate with its arms you must meet it somewhere else. This is not war. If the Spanish commander desires to leave the city and its people, let him surrender and we will then discuss the question as to what shall be done with them."[15] Tedious negotiations followed, but the Spanish were as reluctant as the Americans to face a pitched battle or prolonged siege with the inevitable destruction of the city and loss of life. On July 17 General Toral surrendered, and, for all practical purposes, fighting in Cuba was over.

The Spanish colony of Puerto Rico remained; and in mid-June McKinley authorized an expedition to conquer it, fortifying the belief among friends that he had already accepted overseas ex-

---

[14] Shafter to Henry C. Corbin, July 4, 5, 1898, B. F. Montgomery papers, Rutherford B. Hayes Memorial Library, Fremont, Ohio.

[15] Alger to Shafter, July 4, July 15, 1898, Corbin to Shafter, July 9, 1898, *ibid.*

pansion. On July 25 Miles headed an American expedition to the island, which fell only days before the final armistice.

In Santiago the situation worsened. As early as July Miles warned of yellow fever; and by the first week of August, army doctors reported low supplies of medicine and hospital equipment. On August 2 Shafter cabled urgently that the Army must move to the high ground around Santiago, away from yellow fever's provinces, or perish. The War Department agreed and authorized the move as quickly as transport and living quarters were available in the mountains. But not before the famous "Round Robin Letter" angered the administration and created a sensation among the American people. Roosevelt and a group of officers cabled home that the Army would perish if the War Department did not mend its ways. McKinley was enraged, and Alger was virtually hysterical. They knew that the order to move went out before the officers' letter. But the President did not think it worth a public squabble, and Alger contented himself with a staggering understatement about Roosevelt: "He evidently has little idea of army discipline."[16]

In August and September Army contingents moved into the mountains around Santiago; and the Navy began transporting large numbers of soldiers to the sandy wastes of Point Montauk, Long Island, where a tent city blossomed to house the sick and wounded. Alger was already the butt of public fury at official incompetence, and the President secretly hoped he would resign. But he did not, and McKinley thought it best to stand by him rather than feed him to the wolves of public opinion. That winter a famous commission investigated the ugly charges of corruption and folly that swirled around the War Department's conduct during the war. The commission's report laid the foundations not only for Alger's final resignation, but for a complete reorganization of the armed forces after the turn of the century.

Demobilization promised to be as costly and bitter as mobilization, but in early August McKinley's mind turned to making peace. Indirectly the Spanish had already begun to ask for armistice terms. On July 18 Spain asked the French to state her case.

---

[16] Alger to Charles Moore, August 6, 1898, Alger papers, William L. Clements Library, University of Michigan, Ann Arbor (abbreviated WLCL hereafter).

Due to official delay, negotiations did not begin until July 22, when the French Ambassador, Jules Cambon, hurriedly asked McKinley to outline his armistice terms. Cambon had no sooner left than McKinley summoned his cabinet and advisors to discuss the crucial problem in any armistice: what to do with the Philippines. The President did not force his views, but listened patiently to all, discovering that his cabinet remained divided. Some members wanted all the islands, some wanted none of the islands, and others seemed ready to take a naval station at Manila and leave the rest of the archipelago to Spain. Since General Merritt's army had not yet taken the city, it seemed impossible to claim the islands by right of conquest.

The President now exercised his charm and disingenuous tact. He invited the cabinet for a ride on the Potomac to escape Washington's heat. On a hot day the stiffly attired statesmen embarked on a lighthouse tender for a river cruise where there were no prying eyes or ears. The President heard everyone patiently. Day wanted only a naval base; Treasury Secretary Lyman Gage agreed, but Interior Secretary Cornelius Bliss and Attorney-General John Griggs saw commercial possibilities in taking all the islands. Secretary of Agriculture James Wilson, an old friend and valued political ally of the President's, wanted to evangelize the islands. McKinley laughed, and his eyes twinkled: "Yes, you Scotch favor keeping everything, including the Sabbath."

Cabinet sessions followed on land as the men hammered opposing views into a single policy. Day's first draft of a statement would have retained only Luzon; McKinley buried it. By July 30 personal feelings in the cabinet were giving way; expansion won by a narrow majority when the men voted. After one session Day had remarked: "Mr. President, you didn't put my motion for a naval base." McKinley, who had already remarked that Day only wanted a "hitching post" in the Philippines, replied sagely: "No, Judge, I was afraid it would carry!"[17]

Expansion won in the final tally, though the President deftly left the question of retaining the Philippines open for settlement at the peace conference. Cambon sent Spain the President's outline and tried to soften the blow. The Americans demanded four

---

[17] See Olcott, *William McKinley*, II, 57–75.

points: (1) Spain would free Cuba entirely; (2) the United States would retain Puerto Rico as a war indemnity; (3) the armistice was a suspension, not an end, of hostilities; (4) the Americans would hold the city, bay, and harbor of Manila pending final disposition of the islands at the subsequent peace conference. When the Spanish protested that the United States could not claim the islands on the grounds of conquest, McKinley assured them soothingly that it would be best to leave the matter to the peace conferees. His mind was not made up either way, he said calmly. "The Madrid government may be assured that up to this time there is nothing determined *a priori* in my mind against Spain; likewise, I consider there is nothing decided against the United States."[18] Further Spanish delay was futile, for McKinley would not soften American demands, and Cambon advised Madrid to face reality. The fighting stopped on August 12.

The country was both jubilant and proud of its accomplishments, but here and there men and newspapers worried about the war's results. A Philadelphia newspaper sounded the note among this group by commenting that "with peace will come new responsibilities, which must be met. We have colonies to look after and develop."[19] The Philippine problem remained in suspension, and its solution would open more divisions in American society than the Cuban issue ever had.

McKinley had momentarily met the problem of overseas expansion in a characteristic manner; he left it to be solved at a later conference. He later revealed that this was his purpose all along. He had followed the cabinet's discussions largely to maneuver for support and hear opinion. When the final decision retained Manila and left the rest of the problem to negotiation, the President showed his private secretary a scrap of paper in his pocket on which he had written that exact solution days before. "If the American forces have remained until now in their positions it is in obedience to a duty which respect to residents and strangers and the progress of affairs imposes upon them,"

---

[18] *Spanish Diplomatic Correspondence and Documents, 1896–1900: Presented to the Cortes by the Minister of State* (Washington, D. C., 1905), 216–217 (abbreviated *Sp. Corr.* hereafter).

[19] Philadelphia *Inquirer*, August 15, 1898.

he told the Spanish. It was a roundabout way of saying that the Americans would remain in Manila more or less permanently.[20]

In leaving the Philippine question open to later settlement, McKinley committed his administration to retaining them. Whatever he might infer to the contrary in his few and guarded public utterances, he knew that postponement would develop and focus public opinion in support of his decision to retain the islands. His whole tone as well as his actions indicated that he had made up his own mind. He had annexed Hawaii with allusions to manifest destiny; he had ordered Dewey to the Philippines, knowing what consequences might follow; he had dispatched a land force to conquer those islands; and he had conducted himself during peace negotiations as only an expansionist could. There was only one time at which he could have spurned the Philippines and committed his administration against overseas expansion, and that was the day after Dewey's victory. To delay either way after that merely invited public opinion to "demand" retention. Now that peace had come, he would bide his time, delay proceedings while he sounded the public temper, and subtly maneuver blocs of support into his columns. In the end he adroitly appeared to "capitulate" and accept the islands, just as he had "capitulated" to the demand to free Cuba.

Though relieved by peace, the President knew that his troubles would continue. His own changed status merely symbolized his country's new course. She had defeated a supposedly major European power, thrust herself upon the attention of every government in the world, showed her latent military power, and acquired an empire. It seemed to come suddenly, but the wise man knew that 1898 merely symbolized the end of a very long, complicated, and logical emergence to world power. Old issues were dying, like old men. The country would not be the same again. In McKinley's youth and middle years, a man could enter public life speaking for one great issue, and retire after a long career with that issue still in the forefront of public affairs. The tariff, the currency, the South, internal improvements—all now seemed outmoded. War brought new responsibilities, new problems. He would be the

[20] Olcott, *William McKinley*, II, 64–66; memo dated July 26, McKinley papers, LC; *Sp. Corr.*, 208–209.

first president to have no rest from complicated foreign issues, just as his generation of Americans would be the first to pursue more than "crisis diplomacy." Foreign affairs were here to stay. Responsibility would be the price of greatness.

The war itself was small, glamorous, a thing of charging rough-riders and flashing sabers to many. It was relatively cheap to all save those who suffered and died. But its consequences were far reaching. Placid, insular America was gone. "No war in history has accomplished so much in so short a time with so little loss," wrote Ambassador Horace Porter from Paris. "The nation has at a bound gone forward in the estimation of the world more than we would have done in fifty years of peace," said Senator Proctor. "It is almost a creation or new birth." Such was official opinion, but as usual on such occasions, Mr. Dooley had the best and last word. "We're a gr-reat people," said his friend Mr. Hennessey. "We ar-re that," replied Mr. Dooley. "We ar-re that. An' th' best iv it is, we know we ar-re."[21]

---

[21] Porter to Marcus A. Hanna, August 2, 1898, Porter papers, LC; Proctor to Alger, August 5, 1898, Alger papers, WLCL; Finley Peter Dunne, *Mr. Dooley in Peace and War* (Boston: Small, Maynard, 1899), 9.

CHAPTER V

The Fruits of Victory

THE HEAT OF MID-AUGUST, compounded by pressing diplomatic problems and the war's legacy of confusion and disorder, brought a small but significant change in the President's official family. Sherman's retirement from the State Department when the war erupted brought Judge Day to the premier post as an interim successor, for he did not wish to remain as Secretary of State. He wanted instead the federal judgeship with which McKinley rewarded him later. In tendering his resignation, he remarked jovially to his old friend in the White House that he hated to leave him without his priceless advice at a critical juncture. McKinley laughed in return and remarked humorously that "every change so far in the office of Secretary of State has been an improvement."[1] Day did not escape diplomatic responsibilities, however, for he would now go to Paris as head of the peace commission which McKinley was forming.

Day's successor bespoke the President's understanding of the nation's new foreign responsibilities. In calling John Hay home from London to become Secretary, McKinley served notice that no mere domestic politician would suffice in the post. Hay's long diplomatic record, his foreign travel, and internationalist outlook made him one of the administration's leading spokesmen and one of McKinley's wisest appointments.

The President faced a formidable problem in choosing the commission to make the treaty of peace. He did not think of going himself. No president had yet left the United States on such a

---

[1] Charles S. Olcott, *Life of William McKinley*, 2 vols. (Boston: Houghton-Mifflin, 1916), II, 366.

task, and as a traditionalist he preferred not to challenge long-established precedents. Moreover, he understood the value of remaining at home in contact with party and public opinion; distance would lend objectivity and give the total picture of the peace negotiations.

With a shrewdness that showed his long experience in politics and his understanding of the controversial question of overseas expansion embodied in any peace treaty, the President chose his men carefully. He thought first of sending a member of the Supreme Court, who would symbolize impartiality. But no Justice would enter politics by accepting the burden. He asked Iowa's Senator Allison, a Republican Party stalwart, to be a member of the commission; but he refused, as did several other prominent politicians.

In the end, the President fashioned an admirably balanced commission, and one subtly aligned in favor of his own expansionist policies. Day would go as president, to speak for the administration; his loyalty would mean no quarrel with the ultimate decisions McKinley himself made. To represent the expansionist public and Republicans in general, he chose Whitelaw Reid, publisher of the potent New York *Tribune* and long an ardent expansionist. Three senators would go, testifying to the President's understanding of the nature of ratifying treaties in that body. Cushman K. Davis, chairman of the Foreign Relations Committee, and Maine's William P. Frye would uphold expansion. But it would not do to pack the commission altogether, so McKinley prevailed upon Delaware's conservative anti-expansionist Democratic Senator George Gray to complete the commission. Though his selection of three senators, who would presumably ratify their own work, nettled some members of the upper house, McKinley blandly ignored such objections.

In September, as the commissioners prepared to leave for Paris, domestic politics intruded on the President. Congressional elections were at hand, and the question of expansion and the war's results dominated some contests. Republican failure to win majorities in the new Congress would jeopardize any expansionist treaty made in Paris and throw doubt on the whole idea of overseas expansion. Senator Hanna, national party chairman, urged his friend to enter the local contests; and the President was inclined to use a speechmaking tour to raise support for acquiring the Philippines.

McKinley lacked no advisors that hot summer. Nearly everyone who visited him offered a solution to the Philippine problem. Trends were already evident in many circles. Missionary elements wanted to take the islands and save them for Christianity, conveniently forgetting that they were in large part already Roman Catholic. Pride stirred many newspapers and politicians to retention as a matter of principle; who would now surrender the war's legacy? Though sentiment in the business community was blurred, more and more business spokesmen urged acquisition of the islands as a stepping stone to the supposedly lucrative Oriental trade. By October many businessmen seemed ready to take the islands on economic grounds.[2]

A potentially tense problem confronted the peacemakers in the United States as they devised a course of action toward the Philippines. Foreign ships still lingered in Manila Bay, and intelligence reports from American embassies in Europe indicated a strong interest in many chancelleries over the islands' fate. If the United States did not take them, who would? Could the benevolent Americans return the Philippines to Spain, only to have them fall to Japan or Germany from Spain's feeble grasp? At home the expansionist press did not lessen these fears, and even Senator Hanna modified his doubts about expansion by remarking: "Hoar is crazy. He thinks Germany is just fooling."[3] The Powers would not have risked a war with the United States over the islands, and were never as hostile to American ideas and actions as Americans thought. But was it not logical to assume that the Philippines would pass by default to a hostile nation if the United States refused them? That would be both economically and militarily unwise. In view of all the foreign interest in the Philippines, as

---

[2] See Steiner Brothers to McKinley, August 31, 1898, I. M. Scott to J. B. Moore, August 4, 1898, McKinley papers, Library of Congress, Manuscripts Division, Washington, D. C. (abbreviated LC hereafter). Business sentiment is very hard to judge, but see Julius Pratt, *Expansionists of 1898* (Baltimore: Johns Hopkins Press, 1936), 265–270.

[3] Thomas Beer, *Hanna* (New York: Knopf, 1929), 212.

the President said in his annual message of 1899, the country could not "fling them, a golden apple of discord, among the rival powers."

If the news from abroad fortified the President's desire to retain all the islands, that from home solidified it. While the war raged, McKinley wrote significantly on a scrap of paper: "While we are conducting war and until its conclusion we must keep all we get; when the war is over we must keep what we want."[4] He digested all the intelligence reports and saw confirmation for his belief in many quarters. As early as July, 43 per cent of some sixty-five newspapers polled on the question favored acquiring empire; a mere quarter were undecided, while roughly a third were opposed.[5]

The politicians had their say on the question, and the President kept an open office. In July Western congressmen urged Hanna to speak to him about retaining the islands, feeling that they afforded a rich agricultural market. Others reminded the President that "George Washington has been dead 100 years, and a great many things have happened since his day. . . ." Connecticut's conservative Republican Senator Orville H. Platt spoke for many when he pointed out the position which McKinley had already reached: the realities of diplomacy, power, and responsibility to the natives presented no alternative to retention. "Shall we reach out beyond ourselves, shall we go forward or stand still?" he asked. "If we would maintain ourselves in the front rank we must go forward."[6]

By September, as the time to instruct the peace commission approached, all media available to the President indicated a strong and growing trend toward retaining the islands in the public, the press, and the Republican Party. Anti-expansionists in the party admitted that they were unpopular. "You and I don't want the Philippines," Secretary Long wrote a friend, "but it's no use disguising the fact that an overwhelming majority of the people

---

[4] See Olcott, *William McKinley*, II, 165.

[5] See Richard Hofstadter, "Manifest Destiny and the Philippines," in Daniel Aaron (Ed.), *America in Crisis* (New York: Knopf, 1956).

[6] Beer, *Hanna*, 207; Spencer Borden to McKinley, June 10, 1898, McKinley papers, LC; Louis A. Coolidge, *An Old Fashioned Senator: Orville H. Platt* (New York: Putnam, 1910), 287–290.

do. . . ." Charles Dawes perhaps reflected McKinley's own temper when he wrote flatly: "Whatever the result to our Nation, the retention of the Philippines was inevitable from the first. No man, no party, could have prevented it."[7]

What did the President think? He maintained his silence, listening rather than talking, carefully steering men toward the position his own acts had long since outlined. Allowing men to think they influenced him was his oldest talent, and one which had repaid its use many times in his political career. He followed it once more, listening to Lodge talk of empire and international power, assuring him in noncommittal tones that it was an interesting point. But as early as May, though he thought McKinley was "a little timid," Lodge convinced himself and his powerful friends that the President was in their camp. "I think his imagination is touched by the situation, and I think he grasps it fully."[8]

The President had more to worry about and more to reinforce his silence than his visitors knew. His chief worry focused not in Washington or Madrid, but in distant Manila, where confusion and delay heightened Aguinaldo's suspicions about American designs on his homeland. Would the natives oppose American acquisition, or would they be content as wards of their liberators? No one in Washington could be very sure, for military and diplomatic intelligence reports were confused, often inaccurate, and slow. The first military commanders on the scene thought that conservative Filipinos would welcome American rule if it brought peace and commercial prosperity. The insurgents, they insisted, were only a vocal minority, commanding no appreciable respect among the population. The archipelago consisted of thousands of islands and hundreds of tribes of varying states of civilization, religion, and well-being. Aguinaldo could not presume to speak for them all; his "Republic" was a house of cards.

But the complications were endless. In the year between December 1897 and December 1898, dozens of emissaries passed

[7] Lawrence Shaw Mayo (Ed.), *America of Yesterday: As Reflected in the Journal of John Davis Long* (Boston: Atlantic Monthly Press. 1923), 215; Charles G. Dawes, *A Journal of the McKinley Years* (Chicago: Lakeside Press, 1950), 176.

[8] Henry Cabot Lodge, *The Correspondence of Theodore Roosevelt and Henry Cabot Lodge*, 2 vols. (New York: Scribner, 1922), I, 232, 299–300, 313, 330.

between Aguinaldo and the Americans. There was no doubt that many American diplomatic agents in effect promised the Filipinos that the Americans would free them. If they did not promise outright independence in return for rebel cooperation in ousting the Spanish, they implied it. That the American government always sternly forbade such an understanding made it no less real to those on either side who wanted to believe it.

Aguinaldo often did seem comical. His childish preoccupation with titles and etiquette obscured for many his talents as a leader. "They are big children whom one must treat as little ones," one correspondent wrote McKinley in words he must have rued a year later.[9] The military, though naturally suspicious of any potential opponent, tended to brush aside Filipino pretentions to power. Though singularly opaque in his opinions, Dewey seemed to feel the islanders never wanted independence and would not oppose American rule.

Seeking to clarify his own situation, Aguinaldo sent a trusted advisor, Felipe Agoncillo, to Washington to ask McKinley personally just what his administration intended to do. On October 1 he met the President in his office. McKinley listened to a long recital of Filipino grievances against Spain, delivered tediously through an interpreter. Time passed slowly and the President shifted restlessly in his chair. He made no response to Agoncillo's talk of independence. When he had finished, McKinley tactfully suggested that he leave a copy of his speech which he could study at his leisure. Ten prosy points resulted, and State Department officials took the memorandum from the little brown man with the chilly injunction that this did not imply recognition of his theoretical government.

Mid-September brought both the necessity and the occasion for the President to define his attitude. On the sixteenth of that month, on the eve of their departure for Paris, the peace commissioners assembled at the White House for a farewell dinner and to hear the President's instructions. McKinley talked with them informally and ascertained their views. Day still shrank from a full commitment and thought the United States had slender claim to the islands either by right of conquest or war indemnity.

---

[9] Olcott, *William McKinley*, II, 146, 156.

He would take at most Luzon, the largest island in the group, as a naval and cable station. Reid and Senator Frye wanted all the islands. Davis seemed to favor retaining only part of them. Senator Gray still stubbornly opposed taking any of them. McKinley nodded his head, listened attentively, and said that he felt the people would demand full retention, but did not go further.

The formal instructions which he read his agents held no surprises. The United States did not wish to annex Cuba, he reaffirmed, but would take Puerto Rico as a war indemnity and to end Spanish rule in the hemisphere. The Philippines, he admitted, were a different matter, but the tone of his remarks indicated his belief in the necessity of expansion. The old sound of destiny was there. "The march of events rules and over-rules human action." The least the United States would demand was Luzon, and this clearly would not be enough.[10]

As he bowed his visitors out, McKinley must have thought of how rapidly the scenes shifted. The cables brought problems to him from places he had scarcely thought of a year before. The problems all loomed up, entangled with one another like weeds. From his allotment of precious time he listened to Senator Hanna's insistent voice. Domestic politics could hardly go by default now. The President must enter the fall elections.

McKinley needed only a minimum of persuasion, for he was anxious to sound public opinion on the whole complex question of expansion in the Orient. Late in September the Republican national committee sent him information on local candidates in the Midwest and West, and he announced that he would tour those sections in October. His entry into the elections was little short of historic in an era that did not relish executive interference in local or congressional affairs. With his usual disarming charm, he insisted at every whistle stop that he came not as a Republican but as president of all the people. He moved west in a special train, stopping at crossroads and the principal cities on his line of march, and for two weeks in October spoke to large, enthusiastic crowds. The tour's chief event was an appearance at the Trans-Mississippi Exposition in Omaha on October 12.

---

[10] *Papers Relating to the Foreign Relations of the United States, 1898* (Washington, D.C., 1901), 904–908 (abbreviated *For. Rels.* hereafter).

Speaking in generalities and in a tone of patriotism which few could spurn, he commanded close attention. He tailored his brief, casual remarks to each locality, careful to stress the thing that would give him the most response in that district. Joseph G. Cannon once said that McKinley's ear was so close to the ground that it was full of grasshoppers, and to local politicos who boarded his train at every stop, "the Major" seemed as usual to be listening for the people's voice. Peace, prosperity, a revitalized America were the texts of his addresses. But his subtle references to duty, expansion, and the possibilities of pride and commerce in foreign territory evoked the greatest response. "We have good money, we have ample revenues, we have unquestioned national credit," he told a people basking in unprecedented prosperity and ignorant of foreign complications, "but we want new markets, and as trade follows the flag, it looks very much as if we were going to have new markets."[11]

The tour fulfilled his best expectations, and when he returned to Washington he wrote Whitelaw Reid that it was all "most delightful." And most significant. "Everywhere there were the most enthusiastic demonstrations and the Government seemed to have the hearty support and encouragement of the people."[12] His private callers noted a change in his determination. "None of us have been able to move him since he returned from the west," Secretary Bliss wrote Andrew Carnegie.[13] The stubborn steelmaster, already a bitter foe of expansion, found the President committed to keeping the islands. The people wanted them, he said. Duty called. It was logical and greater dangers lay in rejecting them than in taking them. The November elections pleased McKinley; they were hardly a sweep, but the Republicans would command both houses of the new Congress to assemble in a year.

In distant Paris the cheers surrounding the President's tour came only vaguely through the cables that brought information

---

[11] See *Speeches and Addresses of William McKinley* . . . (New York: Doubleday and McClure, 1900), 109.

[12] McKinley to Reid, October 31, 1898, Reid papers, LC.

[13] See Walter Millis, *The Martial Spirit* (New York: Literary Guild of America, 1931), 383; Lodge to Davis, November 18, 1898, Lodge papers, Massachusetts Historical Society, Boston; Hanna to McKinley, November 15, 1898, McKinley papers, LC.

and instructions to the American negotiators. The French hosts of the conference spread before both delegations a traditional Gallic hospitality. The diplomats of Spain and the United States met in Old World splendor at the Foreign Ministry on the Quai d'Orsay, where spacious and elegant rooms housed their conferences. Though the Americans faced with dread the prospects of tedious discussions with the Spanish, their counterparts seemed to be "men of ability and dignity."[14]

The Spanish hoped to dispose of the Philippine problem quickly; but at the first joint meeting the Americans refused to discuss the issue, since they lacked instructions, and turned instead to Cuba. The disposition of Spanish sovereignty in that unhappy isle consumed the rest of October, as Spain pursued with a grimness worthy of a better cause her hope of unloading the immense Cuban debt on the Americans. Senator Davis fed cigar after cigar into his ash-tray as he sat somnolently and often irritably through long-winded Spanish harangues, and resorts to tedious legal and historical precedents. The steadfast American refusal either to assume the debt or annex Cuba shattered the Spanish belief that the Americans as conquerors would do both, and prolonged their desperate search for something to save face. "The Spanish mind is infinite in its resources . . . ," Day wired home as he read the endless papers that emanated from the Spanish commission.[15] By October 25 the President's patience was exhausted and he instructed the American delegation to move beyond the Cuban debt issue. After informal as well as formal conferences and representations, the Spanish surrendered.

Both parties now turned to the more fascinating Philippine question. Gray still refused to be converted to empire; and Day, though cautious and leaning heavily on McKinley's advice and wishes, seemed committed to retaining nothing but a naval base or at most the island of Luzon. But in the weeks that followed their arrival in Paris, the pro-expansionist commissioners worked on their brethren. By the time the conference turned to the Philippine question, Day was obviously ready to go over reluctantly to the President's point of view.

[14] Day to McKinley, September 30, 1898, McKinley papers, LC.
[15] Day to Hay, October 12, 1898, *ibid.*

Realizing their isolation from events, the American commissioners took McKinley's advice and heard expert testimony when not negotiating. A parade of witnesses passed before them in the afternoons and often in the evenings, answering questions and offering advice and information. General Wesley Merritt spoke with firsthand knowledge of the islands where he had so recently served, and seemed to favor total retention. Like other Army and Navy witnesses, he confirmed the belief that it would be impossible to control only part of the islands. It would have to be all or none.

Admiral Dewey's opinion naturally weighed heavily with both the commission in Paris and the administration in Washington. But Dewey was hard to pin down; now he seemed to favor annexation, now he didn't. As the placid Sundays passed in Paris and the time of commitment drew closer and closer, the positions fell into place. The armed forces favored retaining all the islands. The expansionists like Reid and Frye had but one choice. To the hesitant like Day the argument of duty appealed strongly; the natives were incapable of self-rule and the United States could not simply sail away. On October 13 Dewey had warned that a policy should be settled to alleviate the tension, adding as an afterthought the clinching argument to moralists: "The natives appear unable to govern."[16]

The problem of presidential silence remained. The peace commissioners followed his route across the country in October, reading extracts from his speeches. But they had only a general idea of his reception and purposes. Late in October the President asked the commissioners for their views on the question of annexation, warning that "a very general feeling" in the country dictated that "we cannot let go."[17]

The presidential communication moved Day to activity, and on October 25 he cabled the commissioners' views to Washington. Davis, Frye, and Reid wanted all the islands, feeling that the fall

---

[16] Day to Hay, October 7, 1898; *For. Rels., 1898*, 918–924; Dewey to Long, October 13, 1898, Montgomery papers, Rutherford B. Hayes Memorial Library, Fremont, Ohio.

[17] See Olcott, *William McKinley*, II, 107–108.

of Manila, which was the archipelago's focus, delivered them all by right of conquest. It was impolitic to retain only a portion, and it was impossible to return the islands to Spain or see them lapse by default to another power. Day still favored the "hitching post" of which McKinley had joked. Gray adamantly refused to agree to annexation at all, citing high moral, legal, and political precedents and reasons. He found the allure of empire a trifle hollow in this case. Who could tell what it would cost to rehabilitate the natives? Defense fixtures would be costly, trade uncertain; the Philippines might never repay the cost of their acquisition. He sounded the note that would underlie most of McKinley's opposition in the treaty fight ahead: empire was alien to the American tradition and constitution since it involved governing people without their consent.[18]

McKinley controlled the peace commission with impressive firmness. Though free to argue, discuss, and disagree among themselves, the commissioners knew the President sat near the cable lines that carried their instructions to Paris. He usually spoke through Hay, as decorum and protocol required; but "the President thinks," "the President says," and similar phrases showed his careful attention to every detail of the negotiations. The language in Hay's dispatches was often unmistakably McKinley's.

He insisted firmly on a treaty that would satisfy American claims, but he was not inflexible. His usual tact, insight, and detachment enabled him to compromise and have his way rather than wound Spanish pride still further. In his firmness he risked the rupture in negotiations which the Spanish so often threatened. But he wanted, as he told his spokesmen, a peace "effected in terms which will not only satisfy the general present conditions, but what is more important, be justified in the judgment of posterity."[19] The world was watching American participation in the conference; it would not do to be either harsh or ignorant. Unhappy precedents set here might find a future application against the new world power.

---

[18] *See For. Rels., 1898*, 931–935.
[19] *Ibid.*, 941.

In Washington McKinley read the commissioners' views on the Philippines with interest, but he had long since made up his own mind. While the commissioners talked in Paris, and while he toured the country and then heard advice in Washington, he had weighed both his alternatives and his support. The choices were not happy ones. The people would never leave the islands to Spain. Taking just one island would merely deepen the problem, for divided sovereignty could be worse than no sovereignty. Proclaiming the islands autonomous under American authority was a makeshift which the President rejected, since it implied a shadow responsibility without power to control events in the islands. The only choice open was to take all the islands.

On paper, it was a prosaic decision, but it was not without its drama, as McKinley later revealed. With uncharacteristic self-revelation he told a group of ministers how he had reached his decision. "I have been criticized a good deal about the Philippines, but don't deserve it," he said. He explained that the islands had come as "a gift from the Gods" and outlined his dilemma and alternatives during the summer and fall of 1898. He had frankly thought at first of retaining only a part of the islands. He sought help from all parties but got little support. He was a deeply religious man. After much prayer and thought, it came to him one evening that he had four choices: (1) he could not return the islands to Spain, "that would be cowardly and dishonorable"; (2) he could not turn them over to another power, for "that would be bad business and discreditable"; (3) he could not leave them to themselves, for anarchy and bloodshed would follow in the wake of native ignorance and inability to govern; and (4) so "there was nothing left for us to do but to take them all, and to educate the Filipinos, and uplift and civilize and Christianize them, and by God's grace do the very best we could by them, as our fellow-men for whom Christ also died." His belief in the rightness of this course confirmed the choice.[20]

What the ministers thought of this remarkable statement, they did not say. A later generation, not knowing of McKinley's sincere Christianity, finds it easy to scoff. God, they note, was very clear that night. It is tempting to credit McKinley rather than the

---

[20] Olcott, *William McKinley*, II, 109–111.

Deity with the decision, which is doubtless true. Few of the President's statements reveal so well his thought process and the forces he took into consideration. The statement is a classic outline of his alternatives, but McKinley prefaced them with a disingenuous explanation of how the islands came to the United States. He told many people that he had never wanted them. Yet the suspicion lingers that he knew the train of events Dewey's arrival in Manila Bay would set in motion. No man in politics as long as he could have thought otherwise. Acquisition of the islands was not an innovation; it merely helped confirm the fact of American imperial and economic and political interests in the Orient. Mixed motives produced the demand for the islands: duty to the Filipinos, fear of foreign control, the glittering prospects of trade and politics in the lucrative Eastern markets, and a strong feeling of destiny combined to make acquisition not merely logical but inevitable. Although he was not an emotional man, McKinley found the prospects of American expansion satisfying. In the summer of 1899, he told friends at his home in Ohio that "one of the best things we ever did was to insist upon taking the Philippines and not a coaling station or an island, for if we had done the latter we would have been the laughing stock of the world."[21]

Did he and fellow expansionists understand the only half-hidden prospect of war in the Philippines, the enormous costs of empire, or the cold fact that much of their hope for Oriental trade would prove illusory? Probably not, for they were at the mercy of often erroneous information as well as hard events. To most expansionists, these considerations were not prohibitive. They were willing to risk immediate and temporary costs, believing that long-term results would repay them. America must be great, even if it meant sacrifice.

In Paris the negotiations had almost deadlocked when the President's final instructions to demand all of the islands reached the commission on October 28. The tense Spanish threatened to break up the conference unless they carried home some kind of victory. They must face public opinion too, they reminded their counterparts with considerable justice. They feared their loss of empire might topple the monarchy or provoke disorders in Spain.

---

[21] *Ibid.*, II, 308–309.

Realizing this, Senator Frye had an idea that would soften the blow to Spain and satisfy some adverse public opinion in America. He suggested that the United States pay Spain a sum of money for internal improvements of a pacific character in the Philippines. It would not be an indemnity or bribe, and though some might question the cost, it would be far cheaper than a disrupted conference or even technical continuation of the war. McKinley agreed. "It is the President's wish not only to bring the war to a speedy conclusion, but so to conduct it as to leave no lasting animosities behind to prejudice the future friendship and commerce of the two countries."[22] As usual, McKinley was thinking of the future.

The air was strained when the American commissioners presented their formal demand for all of the islands and indicated that the subject was no longer negotiable. The Spanish commissioners listened with an attitude of "resigned attention" as Day read the statement. When he finished, the Spanish chairman, Eugenio Montero-Rios, jumped up excitedly and asked for a recess while he cabled Madrid.

The wires to Madrid burned with indignation as the Spaniards railed at the American demand. The home government called the demand "the greatest extreme imaginable. . . ."[23] The Spaniards immediately leaped at the loophole in the American claim: they could not acquire the islands by right of conquest since Manila, which fell a day after the official armistice, was not the Philippines. The American delegation was no longer embarrassed by this point; their silence and deadly repetition of a few basic arguments indicated their firmness.

The Philippines had not been as profitable or prestigious to Spain as Cuba. Aside from their vast reservoir of Church converts, the islands did not always repay Spain's investments in them. Spanish control there was somewhat illusory, exercised in large part through treaties and deals with local sultans and native leaders. They had even succeeded once in buying off

---

[22] See the memorandum in Box 213, folder marked "Autobiography: War with Spain, 1898," in John Bassett Moore papers, LC.

[23] *Spanish Diplomatic Correspondence and Documents, 1896–1900: Presented to the Cortes by the Minister of State* (Washington, 1905), 309–311.

Aguinaldo in 1896, a fact that Americans critical of the Filipino leader let no one forget. The Spanish navy found the archipelago indefensible. The army thought it a vast hothouse, to which any officer went with a sense of foreboding and exile. But, as in Cuba, intangible pride played its role. The islands were like the last diamonds of a queen in exile, the more precious in thought for the memories they represented and the illusions they fed. They were "empire," and like Cuba could not be surrendered without a struggle.

The President's firmness and the American delegation's unity, plus the monetary payment of twenty million dollars and a Spanish sense of inevitable doom, brought the end swiftly. In late November the Spaniards capitulated, and the treaty was ready to sign on December 10. To the Spanish it was all tragedy, and the document which they signed so reluctantly was "the pure expression of the immoderate demands of a conqueror who, in order to appear great in history, ought to have made moderate use of its victory."[24] But the Americans naturally saw it from a different angle. The usually restrained and laconic Day, touched perhaps by empire's visions, was unusually ebullient. Their work had brought the country "a goodly estate indeed," he reported home.[25]

In mid-December the President embarked on another tour, this time in the South, which greeted him with a vast display of affection and support. Clearly, he was seeking support not only for the pending treaty but for the expansionist policy it outlined. Just as clearly, he would need all the help he could get, for the fight over ratification promised to be bitter and protracted, and its results were by no means certain.

Within the business community and among certain elements of the administration, the full possibilities of expansion in the Orient became clear only with the passage of the summer's events. By winter a strong current of support for expansion began to emerge from both these groups. For over twenty years many businessmen and diplomats had warned that the nation could not turn blind eyes to Asia. "The opening of the East to Western trade is the greatest fact in the more recent commercial history," the ordi-

---

[24] *Ibid.,* 364.
[25] Day to McKinley, December 12, 1898, McKinley papers, LC.

narily sober *Nation* had remarked in 1882.[26] The war had scarcely begun, and Dewey's victory was hardly official, before at least some business spokesmen began to talk of the dazzling possibilities in Oriental markets, ". . . the balance of colonial power in the China Sea and the possession of the Asiatic markets are equally beyond doubt the basis of European diplomatic controversy as the Nineteenth Century approaches its end," a leading New York commercial paper reported.[27]

Though most administration spokesmen and diplomats were cautious in their views, the possibilities of empire grew clearer and clearer as the summer of 1898 waned. Ranking diplomats and men with experience in the Orient warned against the dangers of failing to compete with the Powers already entrenched there; economics, politics, future power as well as present profit were at stake. From Peking, Minister Charles Denby reported frankly: "I don't like to speak out, but I am greatly inclined to the annexation of Hawaii and the retention of the Philippines. It would be a grand thing for our trade, and ministers in China are forced by circumstances to be commercial agents."[28] In mid-July Secretary Day told John Hay that the war might result in "the need of extending and strengthening our interest in the Asiatic continent."[29] McKinley himself would shortly talk about the "Open Door" in China's trade, suggesting that the new American owners of the Philippines would be glad to trade privilege for privilege to enter the China market. Though in the end he pursued a much more subtle Open Door policy in China in 1900, McKinley was at first inclined to think that if China fell apart the United States "might want a slice if it is to be divided."[30]

These views did not reflect the total opinion of either the business community or of the diplomatic service. Nor was the urge to expand commercially into China the basic reason for acquiring the Philippines; duty and the problems of diplomacy

---

[26] *The Nation*, April 6, 1882, p. 283.

[27] *The Commercial and Financial Chronicle*, 66 (May 14, 1898), 923.

[28] Charles Denby to J. B. Moore, June 10, 1898, Box 214, folder marked "Autobiography: 1896–1900," Moore papers, LC.

[29] Day to Hay, July 14, 1898, Hay papers, LC.

[30] John W. Foster, *Diplomatic Memoirs*, 2 vols. (Boston: Houghton–Mifflin, 1909), II, 257.

were much more apparent and much more important in making that decision. But the prize of Chinese commerce was one of the many forces at work in favor of American overseas expansion.

While these hidden currents worked both for and against the administration's commitment to empire, the Treaty of Paris awaited disposition. "Whatever treaty we get here, I suppose, will meet with considerable opposition from the Senate," Judge Day had wired the President, adding confidently, "but no doubt you are much more familiar with that situation than we can be."[31] As McKinley looked over the Senate that would pass upon the treaty, he saw four basic groups: (1) the administration Republicans favoring its acceptance; (2) the anti-administration Republicans like Senators Hoar and Hale, who opposed it; (3) Democrats who opposed it; (4) and Democrats under the emerging leadership of W. J. Bryan who for varying reasons favored acceptance.

The opposition was worrisome, and even before the treaty was signed, became vocal and bitter in the Senate. Missouri's Senator George G. Vest presented a resolution against expansion on December 6, 1898. Empire, it read, was alien to the American tradition; the nation could not acquire territory beyond her borders not intended to be organized into states. The treaty's opponents voiced a historic American rhetoric that was hard to answer.

Of all the groups that opposed the treaty, the anti-expansionist Democrats angered the President most. Having helped so much to provoke the war, they now refused to share its unexpected burdens. The dissident Republicans had the advantage of familiarity, and of course it was always easier to forgive one strayed from the fold than one who was never in it. But with these varied ingredients in its mixture, the treaty fight promised to be bitter. Lodge's injunction to Roosevelt early in December that "we are going to have trouble over the treaty" did not tell half the story.[32]

Senator Hoar was the President's strangest critic. Long a highly respected Republican regular, and frequently sounding like the supposedly defunct New England Conscience, Hoar would be a serious opponent. McKinley applied his charm in vain; the old

[31] Day to McKinley, November 19, 1898, McKinley papers, LC.
[32] *Roosevelt-Lodge Correspondence*, I, 368.

man would not even consider the offer of Hay's post in London. He was not about to leave the country on the eve of the kind of fight he loved. Asked how he felt, he responded candidly: "Pretty pugnacious, I confess, Mr. President." McKinley took his hand. "I shall always love you, whatever you do." Hoar did not change his mind, for his grounds were of the highest order. "For one I am willing to risk much for liberty," he wrote Senator Chandler in the summer of 1898. "But I am willing to risk nothing for mere empire."[33]

Hoar knew that McKinley was his chief opponent, though he continued to regard him as well meaning. He realized that the administration would use patronage and party allegiance to secure the treaty. Hoar filled many columns in the *Congressional Record* with fine-spun and often sardonically humorous arguments against expansion. And he made some new enemies. "It is difficult for me to speak with moderation of such men as Hoar," Roosevelt said. "They are little better than traitors."[34]

As if congressional opposition were not enough, a formidable body of men in private life rallied to the standard of anti-expansion. Carl Schurz, friend of Lincoln, spokesman for the mugwumps, long a respected figure, bitterly opposed McKinley's ideas. As early as July 1898, he had bluntly reminded the President that "if we annex that island [Puerto Rico] it will be palpable, flagrant conquest by arms, annexation by force, not only unjustified, but undisguised. And what did you say in your annual message? That annexation by force cannot be thought of; that it would be, according to the American code of morals, a *criminal* act of aggression." As he had already remarked concerning Hawaii, "From that time on it would be useless to protest that this is not a war of selfish ambition and conquest."[35]

Such unpleasant reminders were vivid enough in the mail, but the President faced many a formidable critic in equally unpleasant interviews. Andrew Carnegie, a Republican financial

---

[33] George F. Hoar, *Autobiography of Seventy Years*, 2 vols. (New York: Scribner, 1903), II, 315; Hoar to Chandler, July 28, 1898, Chandler papers, LC.

[34] Roosevelt to Lodge, January 26, 1899, Roosevelt papers, LC.

[35] Schurz to McKinley, July 29, May 29, 1898, McKinley papers, LC.

angel when it suited his purposes, hurried to Washington to stop McKinley from taking the Philippines. He found him immovable. Carnegie was not above calling McKinley a tyrant, thirsty for the prestige and power of an emperor. In this he and people of like mind made an ironic judgment. Part of the time they called him weak, and a weathervane for public sentiment; the rest of the time they pilloried him as a tyrant grasping for power, clamoring to command a vengeful army to shoot down helpless men and women. Carnegie's shrill voice rose above the clamor even in October. "Our young men volunteered to fight the oppressor; I shall be surprised if they relish the work of shooting down the oppressed."[36]

To the men around the President, Carnegie seemed mad. "Andrew Carnegie really seems to be off his head," Hay wrote Reid. "He writes me frantic letters signing them 'Your Bitterest Opponent.' He threatens the President, not only with the vengeance of the voters, but with practical punishment at the hands of the mob."[37] Carnegie's real threat to the administration's plans was not so much his voice as his money. His checkbook was a magic wand, as he himself fully realized. "You have brains and I have dollars," he wrote Schurz. "I can devote some of my dollars to spreading your brains."[38]

A curiously varied and incongruous group of men took up the anti-expansionist cause. Carnegie, Hoar, Hale, and Schurz were joined by prominent businessmen like Edward Atkinson; representatives of labor who feared Filipino and Oriental competition; Speaker Thomas B. Reed; ex-President Grover Cleveland; Mark Twain and assorted artistic and literary figures. "What a singular collection the so-called anti-imperialists are getting together," Lodge wrote angrily.[39]

The motives that prompted the anti-expansionists were as varied and elusive as their membership. Many, like Cleveland

---

[36] New York *Times*, October 24, 1898.

[37] Hay to Reid, November 29, 1898, Hay papers, LC.

[38] Carnegie to Schurz, December 27, 1898, Carnegie papers, LC.

[39] See Fred H. Harrington, "The Anti-Imperialist Movement in the United States, 1898–1900," *Mississippi Valley Historical Review*, 22 (September 1935), 211–230.

and Hoar, thought the step unconstitutional and un-American. Some, like Reed, felt the nation had been pushed into war by hysteria and unreasoning jingoism, and saw the question of empire as an afterthought to that action; two wrongs could not make a right. Men like Mark Twain in nonpolitical spheres feared the Republic would lose its vitality and abandon its age-old promises of freedom and liberty if it ruled distant and alien peoples. They belonged to a "little America" school that opposed the "large policy" of making the United States a world power, complete with territorial possessions, dominance of economic markets, and larger armed forces.

Yet their arguments were more subtle than they seemed, and their movement less cohesive than it appeared. They had their flaws of logic. Hoar urged annexation of Hawaii because he thought the people there wanted it. He opposed annexation of the Philippines because he thought the people there did not. The argument that the United States could not acquire foreign territory found fewer partisans in Puerto Rican annexation than in the Philippine question. Those who had always considered the Caribbean an American lake criticized actions there much less than similar actions in the unknown Pacific. They feared the cost and complications hidden in strange lands and stranger peoples in the Orient. To many who opposed taking the Philippines, the principle of annexation was not so doubtful as the territory acquired. Some anti-expansionists shrank not so much from territorial expansion as from war; the means not the ends worried and angered them. They were always willing to extend American control indirectly through trade and peaceful diplomacy, but not through conflict.

Many anti-expansionists favored economic rather than political penetration in the Orient. It was slower but it was cheaper and more enduring. Why annex territory expensive to govern, and laden with unseen but explosive problems of race, religion, and politics? Were the Oriental markets as extensive, or even as prevalent, as their propagandists said? Some of these men thought not. Any generalizations about the anti-expansionists were difficult, but the movement was far more complex than many men thought then and later.

The expansionists' basic motives were simpler. They frankly wished America to behave like the Great Power she was. This required a large Navy, coaling and cable stations, and foreign possessions from which to exercise diplomatic and commercial power. The realities of trade, prestige, and future diplomatic influence were very real to them. This did not mean that the United States must compete with other imperial powers. Almost all expansionists agreed with Senator Lodge that a limited empire in the form of island outposts and bases would suffice. These men did not wish the United States to be another Great Britain, with vast possessions throughout the world. The desire to spread American ideals, so easily pledged in "taking up the white man's burden," sincerely moved many expansionists. They dismissed as absurd the idea that American institutions could not be extended or that empire and world responsibilities would undermine freedom.

Despite the ferocity of the debate around expansionism in 1898, the decision to acquire the Philippines and enter world affairs was not the radical new step its opponents thought they saw. It was the logical culmination of a generation's tendencies in American and world foreign policies. It was "new" in formally recognizing the realities and necessities of America's situation in world affairs. It was "liberal" in promising to extend abroad the best parts of the American ideal. It was "practical" in emphasizing the prospects of trade and political power in world markets. It was "historic" in the broadest sense as the first major step toward the policies that made America a great power in fact as well as potential.

Against the background of these conflicting ideologies, the treaty fight focused in Washington. The most curious man who came to the Capitol in mid-December to aid the treaty was William Jennings Bryan. His contention that the Democrats should accept a Republican treaty took his party off guard, for he was the natural leader of McKinley's opposition. How could he justify accepting a treaty that implemented doctrines he had attacked?

Bryan saw that it would be political folly for the Democrats to defeat the treaty and technically continue the war with all its uncertainties. He thought it wise to remove the issue of expansion from domestic politics so that he could return to free silver, his first love, in the presidential campaign of 1900. "By ratifying the treaty we settled the question with Spain and gave to ourselves the entire control of the Philippine question," he wrote later.[40] Apparently he did not see that ratification would be a blank check for the administration to do with the islands as it pleased.

Carnegie was beside himself with rage at Bryan's interference. The Great Commoner had snatched defeat, he thought, from the jaws of victory and had undone Carnegie's patient and forceful work among the wavering brethren. But Bryan persisted in his labors through January 1899, and apparently aligned several doubtful senators in favor of the treaty.

The senate debates were historic, since they involved constitutional and moral questions of the highest order. Debate started in mid-December, and Orville Platt sounded the administration's keynote when he said: "Providence has put it upon us. We propose to execute it." In the talk that followed he stated McKinley's legal view succinctly: the Constitution implicitly permitted all sovereign acts, including the acquisition of territory.[41]

Hoar's speeches contained a good deal of his celebrated wit, for his innocent face hid one of the sharpest tongues in public life. The President's oft-repeated cry: "Who will haul down the flag?" should read, "Who will haul down the President?" the old man said to a response of laughter and applause. The men now anxious to acquire the islands were remarkable for their ignorance, a Democrat rejoined. "Why, six months ago men who talk that way did not know where the Philippines are."[42]

The debates also brought out a racial argument that had simmered all summer and fall. Many Southerners and some other congressmen opposed taking the Filipinos into the American fold on the grounds that they could not be assimilated. The country had enough racial problems with the Negro in the South and the immigrants in the North. "The experiment of placing the Negro

---

[40] See Paolo Coletta, "Bryan, McKinley and the Treaty of Paris," *Pacific Historical Review*, 26 (May 1957), 131–146; W. J. Bryan, *Memoirs* (Chicago: Winston, 1925), 121–122.

[41] *Congressional Record*, 55th Congress, 3rd Session, 502–503.

[42] Millis, *The Martial Spirit*, 394 ff.

and the white man, side by side, with equal rights, in the South, ought to satisfy everybody of the danger and futility of any further attempt in the same direction," Louisiana's Senator Donelson Caffery wrote Carnegie.[43] Missouri's Champ Clark had already pictured the future of Congress if Hawaiian annexation and the supposed assimilation to follow won the day:

How can we endure our shame when a Chinese senator from Hawaii, with his pigtail hanging down his back, with his pagan joss in his hand, shall rise from his curule chair and in pigeon English proceed to chop logic with GEORGE FRISBIE HOAR or HENRY CABOT LODGE? O tempora, O mores!

How persuasive such talk was is uncertain, but there was such talk.[44]

The tedious arguments over constitutionality did not interest most Americans, but they were susceptible to both logic and emotion. Senator Lodge made a far more telling argument when he appealed to reason and said bluntly:

The President cannot be sent across the Atlantic, in the person of his commissioners, hat in hand, to say to Spain with bated breath: "I am here in obedience to the mandate of a minority of one third of the Senate to tell you that we have been too victorious, and that you have yielded too much, and that I am very sorry that I took the Philippines from you." I do not think that any American President would do that, or that any American would wish him to.[45]

Leadership fell to Lodge, Aldrich, and Hanna, with Stephen B. Elkins playing a leading behind-the-scenes role; and they did not hesitate to use both harsh words and soft promises. The President freely dangled patronage before reluctant senators. Promises of better committee assignments from Aldrich brought over a few wavering votes. Much of this might have seemed unnecessary. The new Senate would be solidly pro-administration, and if the treaty failed of acceptance now, the President could call a special session in March and resubmit it. But that would open breaches in the party and illustrate a division in policy that

---

[43] Donelson Caffery to Carnegie, December 22, 1898, Carnegie papers, LC.

[44] *Congressional Record*, 55th Congress, 2nd Session, 5790–5792.

[45] See Olcott, *William McKinley*, II, 138.

McKinley thought more fictional than real. Whatever the Senate thought, he was sure that the people wanted the treaty.

The President was as subtle as ever, entertaining and conferring with men of all views. His appeals to patriotism were effective, but the more welcome realities of patronage were also persuasive. As February 6, the date set for the vote, approached, Lodge hoped that the two or three votes he might need would be available.

Tension mounted in Washington, but events shifted back to Manila. By late November some American Army officers had warned their superiors to expect trouble with the insurgents, and yet many ranking military officers thought the insurgent threat greatly magnified. Dewey and General E. S. Otis both seemed indifferent to the problem. The War and Navy Departments felt justified in assuming that these commanders in the field knew best. But McKinley's silence toward the Filipinos not only angered Aguinaldo, but convinced him that the Americans meant to demand the islands. The treaty's text, which he read in mid-December, served notice that they would do so.

Filipino leaders found small comfort in vague American assurances about future republican government and cooperation with the local populace. The President held that he could not properly discuss Filipino matters until the treaty was ratified and the islands became American territory. In private, he still hoped to avoid controversy and tension by delaying commitment in the hope of assuring the natives of the administration's good intentions.

It was an unfortunate view, and in the end helped turn Aguinaldo to violence, a path he would doubtlessly have chosen in any event. On January 5, 1899, he proclaimed himself head of the Philippine Republic. On February 4, probably through misunderstanding, American soldiers and Filipino militia fired on each other; and within hours Manila's outskirts echoed to the crack of rifle fire that would punctuate a long and bitter guerrilla conflict.

In Washington McKinley received the first news of the outbreak with dismay, and then with a kind of resigned sadness. "It is always the unexpected that happens, at least in my case," he told his secretary. "How foolish these people are. This means

ratification of the treaty; the people will insist on ratification."[46]
The President went no further, but he said later that he "never
dreamed" the Filipinos would "return our mercy with a Mauser."[47]
To the end of his life, however, he had strong hopes for Filipino
progress, and he always considered the archipelago's inhabitants
second only to the people of his own country.

As the Senate balloted on Monday, February 6, Lodge and other
administration managers watched anxiously; they would need
60 votes if all the senators voted. The results brought them 57,
with 27 opponents. When Vice President Hobart announced the
tally, Hanna rushed through the chamber's doors with his hands
clasped above his head in a victory salute. Lodge felt as if a great
load had passed from his shoulders and congratulated Aldrich
and himself for a job well if not publicly done. "We were down
in the engine room and do not get flowers, but we did make the
ship move."[48]

As McKinley accepted congratulations at the White House,
the Capitol buzzed with talk of who or what had "saved" the
treaty. Some said Bryan did. Others argued that the Filipino
insurrectos did by forcing doubtful men to rally to the flag.
Others argued that public opinion turned the trick. Carnegie
knew that the President had done it. He had used all the arts of
his personality and the powers of his office in a vivid demonstra-
tion of a determined Chief Executive's power. "This is the President's own Pandora's box — this New Year's gift to the country,
for which he is responsible," he wrote Schurz.[49]

Shortly after ratification, the Republicans beat Senator A. O.
Bacon's resolution to grant the Philippines ultimate independence
by Hobart's tie-breaking vote. The President wanted no congressional interference in what he always considered an executive
matter. To McKinley now fell the task of healing party wounds,
and only days after the vote, Hay and Lodge were astonished
to see him beaming over Senator Hoar in his office as if nothing
unpleasant had ever passed between them. McKinley held no

---

[46] Margaret Leech, *In the Days of McKinley* (New York: Harper, 1959),
358; Dawes, *Journal*, 182; Washington *Post*, February 6, 1899.
[47] *Speeches and Addresses* . . . (1900), 216.
[48] *Roosevelt-Lodge Correspondence*, I, 391-392.
[49] Carnegie to Schurz, February 10, 1899, Carnegie papers, LC.

grudges and wisely understood that he might need the senator some day. Hoar still opposed expansion, but left the interview feeling that the President would redeem American promises in the islands.

And so the long and fiery congressional session ended a year of crisis. The nation had passed from uneasy peace to war to empire in that time, and no man could safely predict what lay ahead. The President thought it time to define his policy, at least in a general way, and on February 16 braved a snowstorm to deliver a major address to Boston's Home Market Club. It was a festive occasion despite the freezing chill. Elegant guests covered the great ballroom, half hidden in a profusion of brilliant flowers and flags. Behind the speakers' stand, bunting swathed portraits of Washington, Lincoln, and McKinley. The President made a comprehensive address that outlined the best parts of expansion. He was no racist; he would not condescend to either white man or brown. He did not wish to kill or conquer anyone, and he held out the prospect of peace to the Filipino if he would accept American dominion. In time-honored American fashion, he promised the blessings of material plenty and political liberty to the country's new wards. In closing, he outlined his own vision of what the white man could do with his new burden. The Philippines could become: ". . . a land of plenty and of increasing possibilities; [with] a people redeemed from savage and indolent habits, devoted to the arts of peace, in touch with the commerce and trade of all nations, enjoying the blessings of freedom, of civil and religious liberty, of education, and of homes, and whose children and children's children shall for ages hence bless the American republic because it emancipated their fatherland, and set them in the pathway of the world's best civilization."[50] America's often rough and stony road to empire had brought her to this noble vision and great responsibility. Only the unwritten future could make it real.

---

[50] *Speeches and Addresses* . . . (1900), 185–193; New York *Tribune*, February 17, 1899.

CHAPTER VI

Epilogue

IN THE FEW YEARS that followed the Spanish-American War, Americans often learned more than they cared to know about the problems of empire. They realized with bewildering suddenness that greatness brought unseen responsibilities, and that the status of a world power carried with it grave threats and expenses. The bitter fight over accepting the treaty in 1899 merely symbolized a deep division in American attitudes toward foreign responsibilities.

President McKinley did not live to consummate his plans for Philippine development, for an assassin struck him down in 1901. He did live to develop a plan for semi-autonomous government in the islands, and was always confident of American efforts to rebuild and uplift the islands.

But he and millions of Americans often reflected on the cost of fulfilling the mission they had thought both easy and exalted. Aguinaldo and his rebels fought American control until 1902 in a savage jungle war that threw doubt on the whole concept of imperialism, and raised fresh questions about its costs. As American soldiers in that faraway land, prey to the terrors of climate, disease, and human enemy, fell before the machete and the bullet, some of empire's glitter faded. The trumpet blasts of imperialism and confident talk of destiny and human progress often sounded unreal. As one cynical poet asked:

> We've taken up the white man's burden
> of ebony and brown;
> Now will you tell us, Rudyard,
> how we may put it down?

The soldiers who swung through the jungle laden with heavy packs, in search of an elusive and wily enemy that lived off the tortured land, putting them at the mercy of hidden death a thousand times a day, sang a more bitter song:

Damn, damn, damn the Filipino
Pock-marked Khackiac ladrone;
Underneath the starry flag,
Civilize him with a Krag
And return us to our own beloved home!

But the nation never abandoned empire. Nor did policy makers forget the high charge with which they acquired empire. "I cannot for the life of me see any contradiction between desiring liberty and peace here and desiring to establish them in the Philippines," John Hay wrote a critic.[1] The war's end in the Philippines in 1902 brought peace to the islands, and a modicum of self-government and satisfaction among both the natives and their American rulers. In the half century that followed the United States was true to its promise, and in 1946 the Philippine Republic redeemed that hope of independence. Progress and innovation, success and plenty in the islands never followed any predictable course, but in retrospect the American colonial policy has much to recommend it. Compared to that of other nations, its basic altruism and success is obvious.

In Cuba the Army undertook a program of rehabilitation designed to make the island a showcase for Latin America. In 1902 the Cuban Republic became independent; and the United States hoped that, under a supervision lasting until 1934, its investment of men, money, and time would pay dividends in the future. Puerto Rico remains an American commonwealth, enjoying a peculiar but free status within the American system. Hawaii is a state in the Union, and other Pacific islands enjoy special status under American control.

The broader ramifications of the Spanish-American War carried the echoes of American policies and influence to the globe's far corners. Having acquired the Philippines, the United States

---

[1] Hay to W. A. Croffut, September 28, 1899, Croffut papers, Library of Congress, Manuscripts Division, Washington, D. C.

had interests in China. In 1900 the McKinley administration took the lead in fostering foreign respect of the territorial integrity of that unhappy empire. It also devised the subtle Open Door doctrine that granted American rights in China with a minimum of friction and effort. That it did not endure is less a testament to its inadequacy than to the unpredictability of world events that swept it aside.

America came to empire at the end of a very long and logical process of growth. It was difficult to resist, as the anti-expansionists discovered. The nation's movement toward world power and participation in international events, which the Spanish-American War symbolized rather than caused, carried in it potent ideas and ideals that captured the allegiance of most Americans. It promised to carry the dream of freedom to all the corners of the world; that it did not, that it was often a foolish notion, does not detract from the force of such an appeal. It fed pride in America's greatness; not merely in military or diplomatic might, but in the goodness of her institutions. It bore the hope and partial attainment of profit in the form of trade and commercial expansion. Honest indignation at the thought of misery in other lands, and the earnest desire to end cruelty and oppression, fortified the general public's belief in the American mission. Unpredictable events triggered the responses that made many of these ideas and forces concrete reality.

Both altruism and the needs of a long-term policy of American participation in world affairs dictated the process of expansion overseas. In acting for both these purposes the American people saw no conflict of ideals, for they promised their new charges ultimate self-rule in a democratic system. McKinley eloquently answered those who argued that American ideals would not work in foreign countries, and that empire would sap American freedom. "Nations do not grow in strength, and the cause of liberty and law is not advanced by the doing of easy things . . . ," he said in 1900. "It is not possible that seventy five millions of American freemen are unable to establish liberty and justice and good government in our new possessions."[2] In exhorting his people to ful-

---

[2] *Speeches and Addresses of William McKinley* . . . (New York: Doubleday and McClure, 1900), 361–366.

fill the American ideal of mission, he touched a responsive chord, reminding listeners in his second inaugural: "Our institutions will not deteriorate by extension, and our sense of justice will not abate under tropic suns in distant seas."

Both in intervening in Cuba and acquiring empire, McKinley made the only realistic choices open to him. Those who opposed territorial expansion savored the ideal of an isolated and self-sufficient America that in the facts of trade and diplomacy was already disappearing. Those who wished to extend American ideals, power, and commerce into the Orient and Latin America spoke for a long and steady policy of internationalism. This movement significantly developed under Republicans, as was natural for the party of Seward, Blaine, McKinley, and Theodore Roosevelt. American participation in world affairs was part of the GOP ideal. Though often hidden and subtle, it had been active in American life since the days of Lincoln. Like intervention in Cuba, territorial expansion overseas was an end as well as a beginning.

Once set upon that road, the nation never turned back, though occasional outbursts of opposition to expansion and internationalism reminded America of the bitter ideological struggle of 1898. Perhaps Senator Hoar, who fought so long for his viewpoint, and who was a man of sagacity and humanity, recognized his own opposition best. In 1900 as anti-expansionists prepared to fight "McKinley imperialism" and drive the Republicans from power, the senator shook his head sadly. He knew the American people and the emotions that drew them to the President's side. "The rule of empire, pride in the greatness of the country, the love of the flag and the love of the Republican party, love for the President and the desire to stand by the country in time of war are all motives that touch deeply the hearts of men; and it cannot be otherwise." Though he believed his own ideals would ultimately triumph, he understood the appeal of America's new international status.[3]

A generation more experienced would have expected less gratitude from the peoples it freed and more responsibilities from

---

[3] Hoar to William Claflin, February 17, 1900, Claflin papers, Rutherford B. Hayes Memorial Library, Fremont, Ohio.

the position it assumed. The ease with which Americans faced war and its results in the confident 1890's has faded. And wisely so, for a great nation cannot afford the hazards of overconfidence and rashness. Though the country accepted its responsibilities, doubt gathered around the easy concept of "taking up the white *where & when?* man's burden" that had made empire seem so easy. In time, *with Wilson?* this realization helped bring a fresh realism and hardness into American foreign policy.

Shortly after the war, in his *Devil's Dictionary*, Ambrose Bierce defined the word "zig-zag" as follows: "To move forward uncertainly, from side to side, as one carrying the white man's burden." A more charitable lexicographer would merely have noted that America's road to empire was seldom smooth. In any event, his generation knew what he meant.

Bibliographical Note

Though I have kept my documentation to a minimum, the footnotes reveal my principal sources. The interested reader may wish to pursue the subject further, and I can list here a small number of recent worthwhile works.

Two books dealing with the life and times of President McKinley are vital to any understanding of the problems I have dealt with. Margaret Leech, *In The Days of McKinley* (New York: Harper, 1959), contains a detailed account of the McKinley administration, with special emphasis on the war and its aftermath. My own book, *William McKinley and His America* (Syracuse, N. Y.: Syracuse University Press, 1963), is the only full-length biography of the twenty-fifth president, and contains much more information than I have recounted here.

There are several histories of the period of varying value, but they tend to repeat the same generalizations. The Cuban rebellion of 1895–1898 has had no adequate historian, leaving many critical questions unanswered. Nor has Spain's Cuban diplomacy in those years been detailed in English. Ernest R. May, *Imperial Democracy* (New York: Harcourt, Brace and World, 1961), offers a great deal of information on the attitude of European and Asiatic powers toward the war.

The most famous book dealing with the war itself is still Walter Millis' *The Martial Spirit* (New York: Literary Guild of America, 1931), which is somewhat unfortunate, since it makes the war seem small and often comical. It may be supplemented with Frank Freidel, *The Splendid Little War* (Boston: Little, Brown, 1958). A generation that loved the personal memoir and the hero-worshipping biography produced a flood of more or less ephemeral books on the war. Despite their obvious limitations, they often contain the flavor of the times. The common soldiers' point of view is best seen in Charles Johnson Post, *The Little War of Private Post* (Boston: Little, Brown, 1960).

Albert Weinberg, *Manifest Destiny* (Baltimore: Johns Hopkins Press, 1935), contains some general observations on expansion that are still applicable. The most influential book on the forces at work in favor of expansion in 1898 is Julius Pratt, *Expansionists of 1898* (Baltimore: Johns Hopkins Press, 1936). The book remains full of intriguing information and analysis, though its thesis is open to challenge.

Several younger scholars have done the most provocative work on expansion in recent years. Walter LaFeber, *The New Empire* (Ithaca, N. Y.: Cornell University Press, 1963), offers a general explanation of the whole problem. It is a thoughtful, well-researched, and probing book, marred only by a tendency to overstate its thesis that economic forces motivated American foreign policy in the late nineteenth century. Thomas McCormick, in "Insular Imperialism and the Open Door: The China Market and the Spanish-American War," *Pacific Historical Review*, 32 (May 1963); and " 'A Fair Field and No Favor,' American China Policy During the McKinley Administration 1897–1901" (Unpublished Ph.D. Dissertation, University of Wisconsin, 1960), argues that economic interest in the Asiatic markets promoted American overseas expansion during the whole period. Although it is refeshing to see someone take the men and measures of the era seriously, I feel that business and economic interests were both less cohesive and influential than LaFeber and McCormick. It seems to me that all other things being true, the war and expansion would have come if the business community had been passive or even hostile.

John L. Offner, "President McKinley and the Origins of the Spanish-American War" (Unpublished Ph.D. Dissertation, Pennsylvania State University, 1957), is a thoughtful and detailed study of McKinley's Cuban diplomacy. David F. Healy, *The United States in Cuba, 1898–1902* (Madison: University of Wisconsin Press, 1963), details American work in Cuba after the war.

David M. Pletcher presents useful background information in *The Awkward Years* (Columbia, Mo.: University of Missouri

Press, 1963), dealing with foreign policy under Garfield and Arthur. Milton Plesur offers some thoughtful observations and a great deal of useful information in "Looking Outward: American Attitudes Toward Foreign Affairs in the Years from Hayes to Harrison" (Unpublished Ph.D. Dissertation, University of Rochester, 1954). He also presents a capsule introduction in "Rumblings Beneath the Surface: America's Outward Thrust, 1865–1890," in H. Wayne Morgan (Ed.), *The Gilded Age: A Reappraisal* (Syracuse, N. Y.: Syracuse University Press, 1963).

Many older and more technical works are still useful, and a judicious use of the bibliographies in the books cited here should satisfy the interested reader.

Index

McKinley, President William: 5; on Alger, 70; and American neutrality, 33; and annual message of 1897, 33; on anti-autonomy riots in Havana, 38; appoints naval commission to investigate sinking of the *Maine*, 48; and army appointments, 68–69; and army reform, 68; assassinated, 111; authorizes expedition to Puerto Rico, 78–79; and battle of Santiago, 78; blockades Cuba and calls for volunteers, 67–68; and business interests, 14; on China, 100; on Cleveland's diplomacy, 18; and Congress, 19; and congressional elections of 1898, 86–88; and congressional resolutions concerning Cuba, 20–21; and decision to acquire Philippines, 96–97; and de Lome, 40; and de Lome letter, 42–43; diplomacy compared to Cleveland's, 60–61; as a diplomat, 21–22; and early armistice proposals, 79–80; and early expansionists, 15; and early threats of intervention, 28; on expansionism late in career, 113–114; and Filipino insurrection, 108–109; final armistice demands, 80 ff; and final comprehensive peace plan, 54–55; and final peace treaty, 95; and firm control of peace commission, 95; and first notes on Cuban policy, 27 ff; and first stand on Philippine issue, 75; on Hawaii, 22 ff; and hopes for the Philippines, 110; instructs departing peace commission, 90–91; loses belief in Spanish promises over Cuba, 59; loses popular favor after sinking of *Maine*, 53; and message to Congress on the *Maine* incident, 53; and Oriental markets,

92; Philippine independence, 77; and Philippine question at time of the armistice, 81–82; and political aspects of intervention in Cuba, 55–56; presses for acceptance of Treaty of Paris, 107 ff; and problem of Cuban debt at peace conference, 93–94; and proposed annexation of Cuba, 33; and public silence on Cuban issue, 25–26; receives ambassadors of European powers, 58; receives Filipino emissary, 90; on reconcentration, 8; refuses to remove Lee, 52; and "Round Robin Letter," 79; and selection of peace commission, 85 ff; and Senator Hoar, 101–102; on sending Dewey to Hong Kong, 71; and silence after destruction of the *Maine*, 47–48; and sinking of the *Maine*, 45–47; and speech of Senator Proctor, 51; tours South in winter of 1898, 99; uses *Maine* incident to strengthen his diplomacy, 48–49; and various theoretical solutions to the Cuban problem, 60–62; view on constitutionality of acquiring foreign territory, 106; war message, 57–59; war preparations, 49; and western tour, 91–92; and the yellow press, 14

McKinley Tarriff of 1890: 17

Mahan, Alfred T.: 15

Maine: destruction of, 45 ff; and newspapers, 53; report of court of inquiry upon, 51–54

Manila Bay, Battle of: 72 ff

Maria Christina: 27, 31, 39, 57

Mason, William E.: 19, 34

Merritt, General Wesley: 80, 94

Miles, General Nelson A.: 71; and Cuban invasion, 77, 79

Monroe Doctrine: 3, 9